BRUCE OLDFIELD'S SEASON

WITH GEORGINA HOWELL

PAN BOOKS, LONDON AND SYDNEY

BRUCE OLDFIELD'S

WITH GEORGINA HOWELL

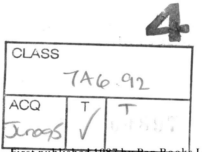
First published 1987 by Pan Books Ltd,
Cavaye Place, London SW10 9PG
9 8 7 6 5 4 3 2 1
© Bruce Oldfield and Georgina Howell 1987
All fashion sketches © Bruce Oldfield 1987
The illustration on pages 65 and 81 © Colin Barnes 1987
Photographs of the Bruce Oldfield company at work © Alan
Wickes 1987
ISBN 0 330 29542X
Set by Rowland Phototypesetting Ltd, Bury St Edmunds, Suffolk
Printed and bound by R. J. Acford

CONTENTS

FOR VIOLET AND SHEILA

FOREWORD

Bruce Oldfield is something that the British fashion
industry badly needs now – a topline designer who is
internationally recognised, a businessman, a media
personality. With all this he is the living proof that you
can make it in Britain, no matter how deprived or
underprivileged your origins, provided you are
talented, ambitious and a workaholic.

Bruce Oldfield's own story is so fascinating that I had
to remind myself continually that this is the
biography of a collection, not the biography of a man.
The story begins on 30 October 1985 at the Interstoff
Fabrics Fair in Frankfurt, where for the first time ideas
meet cloth and begin to take shape in the designer's
mind. Some eighty people then toil for four and a half
months, none harder than the designer and his partner
Anita Richardson, and the collection is finally born in
Fashion Week. No matter what has happened in the
preparation, or what happens in the future, the world's
press judge the collection during those crucial twenty
minutes when the clothes are paraded on the catwalk.
From then on the collection goes on the road: four to six
weeks selling in New York, back to Fulham, three days
in Singapore, off to Vienna to represent 'British
Excellence', and a week in Aspen, Colorado as part of
a prestigious international conference on design.
This year's theme is Britain, and Bruce Oldfield has
been invited to choose and front a mixed show
presenting the best of British fashion designers. The
clothes go into the shop after the summer sales at the
end of August, feeding through until the final bow, the
end-of-season sale at the beginning of January. As
far as the Oldfield company is concerned, this is the
death of the autumn/winter 1986 collection, but for
thousands of women it is only the start of their pleasure
in the clothes themselves. Many will continue to wear
these dresses for fifteen or twenty years, into the next
century, and count the price paid as one of the best small
investments of a lifetime.
You can have worked on the perimeter of fashion for
twenty years, as I have, and still find the business side

a revelation and an education. Nobody who has not
witnessed the day-to-day running of a middle-sized
successful fashion company can have any idea of the
number of conflicting elements that have to be dealt
with simultaneously, or how many problems need
instant solutions in a single day. Fashion designers need
to be Janus-faced, one head turned back to watch the
progress of the collection already in the shops, the other
focused forward on the current collection with its
minefield of deadlines – not just for the clothes, but also
the shoes, hats, bags, gloves, furs, belts, hosiery,
jewellery. There are the licensed lines, the paper pattern
contracts, press previews, international TV
interviews, social and business engagements, private
customers, mega-weddings necessitating trips to
Australia or the Middle East. There are company
conferences with Anita Richardson, sessions with the
accountant, licensing deals to be considered, expansions
to be projected and pondered, tributes to be gracefully
accepted. In the run-up to the show Bruce Oldfield
was voted Northern Personality of the Year in
Newcastle and designer of Dress of the Year in Bath.
And there are, always, the interruptions that interrupt
interruptions.

Bruce Oldfield was determined that this should be a
no-frills businesslike book about running the
business. Just as David Bailey finally persuaded the
world back in the early sixties that you don't have to
'have your head in a cloud of pink chiffon' to be a
fashion photographer, Bruce Oldfield's success
should convince the public that you don't have to be a
whimsical prima donna to be a fashion designer.

Georgina Howell

1

BRUCE OLDFIELD BIOGRAPHY

'IT WOULD PROBABLY HAVE BEEN BETTER FOR ME TO HAVE LIVED AT AN EARLIER PERIOD, BECAUSE I CARE ABOUT THE TECHNIQUE OF MAKING CLOTHES. I LIKE A GOOD GARMENT. I'M INTO THE TECHNICAL SIDE.'

1950 Born 14 July in Hammersmith Hospital, London, the illegitimate son of a white mother from the London area and a Jamaican boxer. Stays in Hammersmith and Great Ormond Street Hospital for Sick Children for six months, then to a children's convalescent home in Bognor Regis until nine months old.

1951 Taken into care at nine-months old by a Dr Barnardo nursery home: Roberts House, Tewit Well Road, Harrogate. Fostered at eighteen months by tailor and dressmaker Miss Violet Masters of the village of Hett in County Durham; joined by his foster brothers George (half Indian) and Barry (half Nigerian). Later additions to the family were Linda (half Malay) and Janet (half Jamaican).

1955 Educated at Dean
-1963 Bank Infant and Junior School, Ferryhill, from five to eleven years old, and Spennymoor Grammar Technical School from eleven to thirteen.

1963 Aged thirteen, removed from his foster family and returned to a Dr Barnardo branch home, West Mount, Ripon: continues his education between 1963 and 1968, aged thirteen to eighteen, at Ripon Grammar School, Yorkshire, where he takes his A levels.

1968 Begins a three-year teacher training course at Sheffield City College of Education.

1971 Moves to London to take a Fashion and Textiles degree course at Ravensbourne College of Art and Design with the help of a grant from a Dr Barnardo's trust fund for further education.

1972 Transfers in mid-term to St Martin's School of Art to study fashion. Wins the Saga mink competition and is commissioned to design the clothes for Revlon's 'Charlie' promotion in Europe.

DENNIS PIEL/*VOGUE*

1973 Leaves in June to design collections for Liberty and Choses of Sloane Street. Only three months later he is invited to New York by Henri Bendel to design an exclusive collection for them. His first solo show is held at the Plaza in November.

1974 Returns to London and concentrates on wholesale collections for Browns and Tsaritsar. Spends seven months in Paris working freelance: among the commissions, sells shoe designs to Yves St Laurent.

1975 Sets up his own company in London with a £1,000 bank loan and a further £500 loan from Dr Barnardo's. Makes wholesale collections from Shawfield Street and, later, Walton Street. Sells his first collection to Harvey Nichols,

Wardrobe, Chic of Hampstead, Saks Fifth Avenue, Bloomingdales, Elizabeth Arden and Bergdorf Goodman, among others.

1976 Produces two
-1977 ready-to-wear collections a year and works on special projects, such as a film wardrobe for Charlotte Rampling for *Le Taxi Mauve* in the South of France. Designs a menswear collection for a British fashion spectacular in Venice, and shows his first West Coast collection in Beverley Hills, California.

1978 Moves his business
-1983 to 41 Beauchamp Place and begins to build a private clientèle in tandem with the ready-to-wear collections which, by the early eighties, sell through the world's most exclusive stores and boutiques. Special projects include a film wardrobe for Joan Collins in *The Bitch*. An increasing emphasis on the private customer leads to the decision to concentrate on providing

an exclusively couture service by 1983, making unique and glamorous evening dresses and wedding dresses.

1984 Opens the first Bruce Oldfield shop in June at 27 Beauchamp Place, London SW3, opposite the original workroom, selling a total look from one London showplace. Simultaneously through a New York agent he shows a wholesale collection while continuing his private couture business.

1985 Gala fashion show in March in aid of Dr Barnardo's, with HRH The Princess of Wales, president of Dr Barnardo's, as guest of honour. Show raises £104,000 for the homes. A Bruce Oldfield dress is chosen as Dress of the Year by Suzy Menkes, Fashion Editor of *The Times*, and put on permanent display at the Museum of Costume in Bath. Bruce Oldfield is picked as Northern Personality of the Year by the Variety Club of Great Britain. In September, he turns

ALEX CHATELAIN/ *VOGUE*

down the design directorship of Norman Hartnell, dressmaker to HM The Queen Mother.

ERIC BOMAN/*VOGUE*

'NOTHING'S FOREVER,
NOTHING'S DEFINITE
AND THE PUBLICITY
MEANS NOTHING.'

TONY McGEE

INTERVIEW

When were you first aware of being poor, black and illegitimate?

Poor? I never felt hard done by, except that if you're in care there's always this element of money. My foster mother was paid to look after me and she never got enough so there were problems. But it was nothing like the rows that came later when I was seventeen and living in lodgings while I took my A levels. I lived with a family with whom I had continual problems about money.

Black? I'm sure that was brought home to me in some way fairly early on. I remember when I was six we went with our foster mother to the Durham Miners' Gala, and while we were waiting for a bus this crazy woman with a stick came up the road and whacked Violet across the backside and shouted out, 'I had a dream, and in the dream God told me that black children shouldn't be here. They should go back to Africa!' That I remember. But we were rather lionised up north, you know. We were cute little piccaninnies all dressed the same in colourful shirts and the thick tweed trousers our foster mum used to make us.

Illegitimate? Probably never occurred to me until . . . I really don't know.

How much do you know about your parents?

We–ell, I know that my mother was of dubious morals, or that it seemed that way in the fifties. Probably not true in relation to the eighties. My father was a boxer. That's as much as I know, and in a way as much as I care to know. In my early twenties I was more curious about them. Every time my birthday came round I would set myself the task of finding out a little bit more. I even went to Hammersmith Hospital once to go through the records, but that proved to be a dead end. When I was at Ravensbourne I stuck my birth certificate into a scrapbook and wrote something pretentious underneath like '. . . and he just went on from there.' Yuck! But you do things like that when you are at art college. So if someone turned up one day and said 'I'm your mother', I must say I would be most annoyed. Who needs the aggravation? My foster mother was my mother. At my age I certainly don't want the responsibility of a mum or a dad.

What is your first memory?
It's a flashback. When I was about sixteen I went to some kind of social gathering in Harrogate for Dr Barnardo's children in the area. I walked into this home and I had an intense feeling of *déjà vu*. I remembered everything I saw in the house, and I knew that if I went outside I would see something like a bandstand and that somewhere there was a railway line. So I went into the garden and at the bottom there was the railway line and just beside it there was a domed building like a folly. It was the house I lived in from nine months to eighteen months. So I was obviously an observant little bugger, even at the age of one!

Your foster mother was a dressmaker?
Violet was an outworker and a private dressmaker, and she did it to survive. She fostered seventeen children over the years – I overlapped with six of them. Her work was going on in the house all the time and she made all our clothes, so we couldn't help but pick up a sense of cutting and sewing. But I was probably the most interested. I asked more questions so she told me more than the others. When I was thirteen or fourteen she would show me whatever she was doing, and I would look at the cloth: I had a feeling for

how it would drape and fall. I'm sure, looking back, that Violet knew I would end up as a fashion designer, but then, up north in the late fifties and early sixties, fashion design wasn't one of the options. Violet made a creative atmosphere for all of us. We would always be making or painting something. We would have a train set and she would get us all making *papier mâché* mountains and tunnels for the train to go through.

Was there a point at which you became too much of a handful for your foster mother?

We were three teenage boys living with a single woman who was probably much nearer sixty than fifty, but had lied about her age: a handful, and I was the worst. The crunch came when she found out we had been shoplifting. Yeah, I was brilliant at it, came home with Superman comics and sweets. I thought everyone did when they were kids. Then a few years ago the *Sun* picked up on it. 'Fifteen things you didn't know about Bruce Oldfield! Used to be a great shoplifter!' Bloody hell. Next thing a German newspaper spreads it all across a page, 'Di's darling cutter was a shoplifter!'

How did it come about that you left Violet and went back to a Dr Barnardo's branch home?

Well, if you're deemed to be out of the control of the person who's looking after you, then they take you back. My foster mother felt she couldn't handle me . . . When you were at Barnardo's you were always aware that the next step down was Borstal. When you went to your foster mother you were told, 'If you don't behave yourself you come back into the Home.' Right, so then I went back to the Home. Then, at the branch homes, their recourse if you make trouble was to say, 'If you don't behave yourself now we'll make you a ward of court.' Then you had to behave yourself because you were under the jurisdiction of the court. So that was the atmosphere in which you were brought up. If you didn't shape up there were always penalties just around the corner. Possibly that's what makes me aggressive.

You said once that Barnardo's heavy-handed rules and regulations made you strong and confident. What did you mean by that?

There's no room for stars in an institution, there has to be one rule for everybody. And I didn't get on very well with the superintendent. When I was working for my O levels and my A levels, and I was the only one there who was at the grammar school, I felt I deserved a room to myself to work in. Particularly as I was sharing a room with a slightly retarded fourteen-year-old when I was sixteen. So I started demanding what I considered to be fair dos, and I had to be fairly boisterous to get the room. But I got it. All the other kids went to the secondary modern which was on the other side of the road from the grammar school, and there was a lot of flak. And the superintendent's son went to the secondary modern too . . . But you just get on with it, don't you? It was much the same when I went to St Martin's. I would walk into the third year lectures in my second year, and win prizes, and refuse to do easy class projects. At Barnardo's I suppose I took a fairly selfish line. You keep your side and I'll keep mine. Dealing with my peers, I don't think I used much charm.

What were the long-term effects?

I suppose it made me a loner. I've always gravitated towards people slightly older than myself and I have never had much patience with my peers. I'm not a sportsman and I don't much like group activities;

teamwork has never been my strong point. I would
never be a football player – unless I could be team
captain! Having drinks with the lads has never been
my scene. I never understand how problems can be
solved in group meetings. The way we do things here, if
something has to be discussed, is that I ask everyone
concerned if they will write down the five points they
think should be considered, someone types the whole
lot up and then we have a quick meeting.

*You have done an awful lot for Barnardo's. Do you feel you
have repaid your debt?*
I don't think of it in those terms. I have a very soft spot
for them. When you are there and you leave, you don't
rate Barnardo's very highly. You think, what the hell
do they know. But when I moved to London they gave
me the grant, and when I started my business they
loaned me £500. I did get the feeling then that I had
been *slightly* ungenerous and mean-spirited about
them.
I think there were some very bad things about the way
we were brought up and the way they looked at child
care in the fifties and sixties. In my time there were
twenty-five boys under one roof, three to seventeen
years old, and all slightly disturbed, probably
including me. It was very institutionalised, and it was
bound to be rough justice. When I was at Ripon there
were only two of us who had made it to grammar school
among 8,000 Barnardo kids. Since then it has all
changed. The large branch homes have been closed, and
now it's based on small groups, say five boys with five
staff to look after them, which is as it should be. And for
various reasons there are fewer kids in care anyway.
Barnardo's now take in only handicapped children.
Most of the kids who came out of Barnardo's at the end

of the day were pretty . . . well, I don't know how many turned to crime, but it was a fairly delinquent, underprivileged group. I don't know how many made anything of themselves. Anyway, I feel I have a sort of responsibility to Barnardo's. I can't complain for myself because I turned out OK, I suppose.

One of your workroom ladies told me that when you were just starting out she asked you what you wanted to be, and you replied 'Famous'.

At eighteen I decided I was going to be a huge success. But I wasn't sure what at! And in a way, as long as it was something creative, I could have turned my hand to quite a few careers – design, acting, architecture – if I had had the training. So although I love what I do, and do it well, I'm more committed to success with a capital 'S' than to fashion.

I have this driving ambition. I don't know where it comes from but it carries me along. I've always aimed at the best I knew about, and when people told me I couldn't get there I took particular pleasure in proving them wrong. When I was at teacher training college I thought the people I was with seemed a little narrow, their aspirations quite low, so most of the time I was elsewhere. Then I applied to art school and I got in, much to the annoyance of all the people who said I couldn't do it. Then they said I wouldn't get a grant. So I wrote thirty letters to different industries, to Courtaulds and all the biggest institutions, and I eventually got a grant from Dr Barnardo's. Then when I was at Ravensbourne I realised pretty soon that the place to get yourself noticed was St Martin's, which was watched quite closely by the press and which was a much more PR-oriented college. There were journalists coming in all the time to give talks. So I applied to St

Martin's and everyone said 'What makes you think you're so special? You'll never get a transfer.' And the principal of St Martin's wouldn't take me. She wrote to say it was mid-term and, in any case, they were full. So I went down to St Martin's with my portfolio and tried to see her, and wasn't allowed to. I said 'OK, I'll come back tomorrow.' Went back the next day. Waited for hours. Then she said 'OK, for God's sake, I'll see your stuff.' And when she had seen it, she said 'You start on Monday.' And that's how it has been all along.

How did you find a sense of direction?
Through work. I liked school, although I wasn't a high achiever. I did not like being in Dr Barnardo's, I did not like West Mount, the branch home, and I didn't like before nine, after four, or weekends. School was normal, I guess. Teacher training college wasn't a great strain on my resources. I got by on the minimum of work, and had a great social life. I suddenly became much more confident. My school teachers had advised me to take a teacher training course and I chose English and art as my subjects. The advice turned out to be useful, because the course not only taught me to teach, but also to extend my ideas in the field. I also designed textiles, but it seemed rather pointless unless you carried it through and made clothes out of them. I had a friend at the local university, a Nigerian girl, and I made her some dresses out of my fabrics. I'm sure I made them in a rather ham-fisted way, but she liked them, and made them look rather good.
When I was in my second year of teacher training, my foster brother, Barry, was living with me in Sheffield. We were running rather a profitable little business in the summer holidays. We would buy ten 2s 3d tank-tops

in Tesco, dye them and print them, and resell them for 7s 3d. I was the salesman and I soon had a bookful of contacts in small shops round the Sheffield/Leeds areas. All these straws in the wind told me that my real interests lay in the direction of fashion design. In any case, I was already spending all my free time with the local art students. And then, when I was teaching kids as part of my training, my tutor asked me why I patronised them. It was an eye-opener. I suddenly realised that at the back of my mind I wanted to get out into the world and do more than teach. When I got to Ravensbourne, I was a real swot. I worked and worked and worked. I knew I was aiming in the right direction, and by the time I got to St Martin's I was self-directed. I was a pain in the neck. I wouldn't do their projects, because I thought they were too easy or just daft. 'Who the hell wants to design six dresses around the bicycle?' I would ask, or 'Who wants to sit and stitch two sorts of pockets on to a duster? I'll make you a jacket which has a collar, one patch pocket, one welt pocket and a sleeve set in. I'll do the whole damn thing. That way I'll learn.' They treated everyone the same, which is to say that everyone was at the same level of competence. Well, some of us were just a little bit beyond those class projects. After two years there I had a collection and I asked if I could leave. They were happy to see the back of me. What would have been good for me, with hindsight, was to go off to Paris and work for Yves Saint Laurent, or Dior, for a couple of years and learn more about the craft.

When Bendel's invited you to New York to design a collection for them you had only just left college. How did they hear about you?
That nonsense with Bendel's! At St Martin's I had

been written up by Judy Brittain of *Vogue*, and then
Joan Buck from *Women's Wear Daily*, the influential
American fashion newspaper, had come in to give a
lecture to the third year students. And in my usual
uppity way I cruised in and interrupted and kept asking
questions. I had just won a competition and been
chosen to do the clothes for the 'Charlie' promotion,
and Joan wrote a piece about me. That's how I came
to the notice of Geraldine Stutz, the president of
Bendel's. One day I was at home in Brixton and I was at
the Hawaiian shirt and shorts stage, wearing green
plastic sandals, and suddenly up the street slid this big
white Daimler. This *enormously* chic woman in a turban
and silk shirt and pants got out and came upstairs. It was
like Greta Garbo sitting in your front room. She said,
'Would you like to come to New York and design a
collection for us?' 'Yeah, sure, great!' The next thing I
was on a first-class flight, staying at the Plaza, with
limousines to pick me up and $200 a day for pocket
money.
The first three weeks I didn't do a damn thing. I had
never worked for anybody before, I had never been in a
work situation. I didn't know what was expected of me.
It was my first glimpse of New York and I found the
nightspots quite quickly and got into bad habits.
Eventually I did a few drawings and the production
man had a look, and said, 'They're nice, but we're not
going to be able to make them.' So that worried me. The
same day Geraldine Stutz came in, saw a toile, and said,
'That's good.' 'Yes,' I said, 'but will it sell?' She bristled
up and replied, 'See me in my office', doing a Barbara
Stanwyck number. So I went in and she railed at me:
'Never let me hear you say that again. A designer
shouldn't worry about whether something will sell!'
Ironical, really, in view of what happened later . . .

Even at that age, whilst I knew that commerce shouldn't override creativity, I did know that it should be considered. But at twenty-three, what do you do? Anyway, there was a spurt of action and ten things got made. On the basis of that they asked me to stay another couple of months and work on a proper wholesale collection. As far as I was concerned, I had a job. I did the show at the Plaza within four months of leaving college, and then I felt slightly silly because the collection didn't sell as much as they had wanted it to sell. They have targets which have to be reached by certain dates, and they don't give any room for development or growth, so if you're not an immediate success, forget it. I wasn't an immediate success, so they forgot it. I'd been chasing the lease for an apartment on Fifth Avenue. When they got to hear about it, it was, 'Oh, erm, Bruce, don't take that lease – you won't be here much longer.' I came in a limousine, and went back by bus.

As far as Bendel's were concerned, they had given me a fantastic break. From my point of view, I learnt an important lesson, and I'm glad I learnt it right at the beginning of my career. What I learnt was not to believe the hype. All the time I was there the *New York Times* and *Women's Wear Daily* were calling me 'Bendel's new iron in the fire' and 'Top designer Bruce Oldfield'. Top designer? I wasn't even sure what they wanted me to do! I learnt that nothing's forever, nothing's definite, and the publicity means nothing.

You were a rising star in the seventies.
Yeah – but I call it premature adulation. I had many false starts. I started my own business in 1975, and Anita Richardson joined me when Tsaritsar closed. At Shawfield Street and Walton Street we ran the whole

thing from a couple of rooms, on a shoestring. We were
cutting out on one end of the table and doing sums at
the other. I went to New York, selling to
Bloomingdales and Barneys and so on. We were always
expanding and contracting. If the collection was
selling well we needed to take on more people. If it
wasn't, Anita and I would sit on a bench in Hyde Park and
work out who we could sack and which part of the
property we could lease off. I once sold a lamp to pay a
machinist. The mid-seventies to the eighties was
growth and retrenchment, growth and retrenchment.
That's what was going on behind the scenes.

What happened when you opened your shop in Beauchamp
Place in June 1984?
I had wanted to do this for a long time, and then
premises became available just opposite our workroom.
I didn't like the feeling that once I had finished a
collection, it slid right out of my hands. It gives me a
terrific buzz every time I walk into the shop and see a
woman trying on one of my dresses, and more so when
she actually purchases it. It's nothing to do with the
clack of the American Express card. I like to see the whole
process through, and it gives *me* a kick that *she* is getting
a kick out of a Bruce Oldfield number.
Now we've got three strands running simultaneously –
the wholesale, ready-to-wear collection, home and
export; the private customer collection; plus shoe,
tights and fur collections, and other licensing
ventures. The shop did so well last year that we were
able to expand and take over large premises in Fulham
for workroom, studio and offices.

How did you move from wholesale to couture?
It started off back around 1980, before the royal
wedding, when there was a great divergence between

what people saw in magazines and what they could actually buy in the shops. We would present a collection, the stores would make their selection and the press would pick up on the new looks. The trouble was, the two didn't coincide. The stores would buy the safe numbers, the garments they knew they could sell, the things you were known for. The press would pick the things that made the strongest pictures. So the pink taffeta ballgowns were featured, but you couldn't buy them. We started getting a lot of phone calls and decided to make for those customers privately.

During that period I was reacting against the apparent disregard for quality and workmanship that was developing in wholesale dress manufacturing. This is not to say that I think everything should be heavily interlined or carefully handstiched and individually made, but I felt there was a certain sloppiness being accepted by retailers, press and customers under the guise of a new look, and I didn't want to be part of it. While I was expanding my repertoire and producing more dressed-up clothes, the rest of London seemed to be catering for the dressed-down market. My press profile in some seasons was very low indeed! The majority of merchandise featured in the magazines, outside of my unavailable gowns, was downbeat or American classic, and I believed the emphasis on such styling came from isolated editorials. So the customer came knocking on my door for something more special.

It would probably have been better for me to have lived at an earlier period, because I care about the technique of making clothes. I like a good garment. I'm into the technical side. Nowadays, with the pressures of keeping prices to a certain level and getting things out on time, it's a battle to maintain the highest standards. It's because of the standard of workmanship you produce for couture that I was attracted to the private client. You are actually considering the woman in the dress rather than an unknown quantity who walks into a department store and buys a dress off the peg. Those customers I had been making evening and wedding dresses for privately were an incredibly important means to an end, and a vital part of the learning process.

Are they still?
As the business builds and more things take up my time I have to cut down on private clients, and the off-the-peg side is a bigger money-maker. Now that we have new workrooms we've cleared a section of the shop for made-to-measure. I design a group of clothes for the clients that will be made strictly to order. The sales staff and fitters, and occasionally myself, can adapt those designs to suit the individual client's requirements.

Recently, HM The Queen Mother's couturier, Norman Hartnell, invited you to become their design director. What went through your mind before you turned down the job?
I never thought of accepting! I have built up my business for ten years and it has a long way to go: the shop by then had only been open for a year. I would have had to set up the whole workroom structure at Hartnell – that salon is 11,000 square feet of the choicest property in London with a royal warrant, but there were just six floors of nothing. I would have been there eight days a week. *The Times* ran the story that I'd been offered the job and a public decision had to be made. Then Hartnell panicked and denied that I had been offered it, which annoyed me. So I had no option other than to issue a press release to say that, although flattered, I would not be taking the job.

Who is the typical Bruce Oldfield customer?
She is expensive, sexy, body-conscious, like my
clothes. Age group twenty-five to sixty. She's a
middle-class woman in good shape, often doing a job,
sure of herself. She doesn't want outrageous clothes.
She's not a walking fashion plate. She's a great-
looking woman in a flattering dress. Her clothes bills
are possibly paid by a man. I can make any woman
look better. That's what I do. After all, I have fitted ten
figures a day for three years – you get to know how.

How would you sum up the Bruce Oldfield style?
I don't often analyse my style, so it's the thing I can talk
least eloquently about. When I left college the fashion
stars were Zandra Rhodes, Bill Gibb, Gina Fratini,
Yuki, John Bates and Jean Muir. Those six. And with
the sole exception of Jean Muir they all made fantasy
clothes. Crazy fashion was very popular at college, and
I could draw fantasy clothes, but they never
convinced me. I am very conservative by nature and my
clothes are not overstated. I can understand fantasy
as a bit of theatre for the runway, but I like to make the
kind of clothes that people wear. So I ignored all that and
I came in with the mid-seventies wave who were
beginning to make fairly simple things – people like
Adrian Cartmell and Sheridan Barnett. There have
been times when I have been in fashion and times when I
have been out of fashion, but I have always had six pages
a year in *Vogue*, sometimes fifteen.
Looking back through old sketchbooks, I see to my
surprise there is an identifiable Bruce Oldfield look,
to do with proportions and coloration. And it has
longevity. There must be fifteen people who have
told me recently, 'I'm still wearing a dress I bought
from you eight years ago'.

What next?

I don't aim at more and more money. It seems to me I
already live well: OK, I could have a better flat, a bigger
car, but money has never been my prime motivator.
Yachts bore me, I get restless at Annabel's, I leave the
races early to go back and work. Or I listen to music and
read. I don't like staying up too late.
Yeah, I'd like an empire. I want a shop in New York –
it's under discussion at the moment. I want my name
on expensive sheets and stockings, I want retail outfits
dotted around the world. It's all part of the Bruce
Oldfield development plan. If you build up a mega-
business like Ralph Lauren, Calvin Klein, Cardin or
whatever, then you do influence people. I don't believe
there's a great deal of mileage in being known merely
as a fashion designer. The label suggests someone
lightweight and impermanent. Fashion is of now, and
it can be over in five minutes. I'm equally interested in
being a businessman as I am in being a fashion
designer. I find it enormously satisfying to run the
company and know that it's shipshape, expanding
and that we have a good team who will stay with us. I
get a lot of pleasure from knowing that we'll be here
next year and the year after that and the year after
that . . . I also enjoy the part of the job that benefits from
my being known as a real person, both to my clients and
the public at large. I've got an outgoing personality
and I'm told I'm fairly good on the box, presentable and
quick-talking. Some designers, however bright they are,
talk . . . so . . . slowly . . . they . . . bore . . .
you . . . to . . . death. I can use all that to build the
business and make it less vulnerable to the vagaries of
fashion.
Yes, I could handle an empire.

THE BRUCE OLDFIELD COMPANY: *Cast List*

3

ANITA RICHARDSON

GEORGINA ALEXANDER-SINCLAIR

CHRISTINE FOX

JUDITH WOLKENFELD

LYNNE SOLLIT

LINDY GIBBON

ERIS CROSS

EMILIA ESPINOSA

MARIE TODD

NEILA SOUISSI

MARGARET CARTER

ROSALIND WOOLFSON

Anita Richardson,
partner

Born in Oxford and educated in London, her first job in fashion was liaising between buyers and manufacturers for an international retail organisation. 'That's where I got the bug for this business.' As well as giving her a good start in the fashion industry, it taught Anita the importance of deadlines, of working towards delivery dates on a large scale.

She first worked on the manufacturing side at Angela Gore, by contrast a small business: 'This was my most important and formative early work experience. In a small company I was doing everything, dealing with press and buyers, putting on shows, controlling production; in fact, it was a foretaste of my work with Bruce. I left Angela to the designing, and got on with the business side of things.' She worked with Angela Gore for four years, and after other jobs her talent for organisation and administration took her to Annette Worsley-Taylor's company Tsaritsar, where she ran the wholesale side of the business. She met Bruce Oldfield, still a student at St Martin's, when he brought in his work at the instigation of Tsaritsar's press representative Liz Shirley. The two started out on their own in 1975. 'I was pregnant at the time. I think he probably reckoned I wouldn't be around for too long!

'We showed Bruce's first independent collection in March 1975, and within a week we had £30,000-worth of orders from home and the US.'

Anita arranged the initial overdraft allowance from the bank. She and Bruce spent the money on fabrics, made a batch of garments and 'sent them to the companies we knew paid within a week. Then we used that cheque to pay our workers and invest in the next lot of fabrics.'

After one season, Hill Samuel were impressed enough to grant the company a larger overdraft, and within a year they had a workroom and showroom at 9 Walton Street, South Kensington SW3. They had expanded into two floors at 41 Beauchamp Place with ten employees before they realised they had over-stretched their resources too early. From 1979 onwards talent and careful organisation has brought the company to its present stable position, the landmarks being the opening of the shop in June 1984, and expanding the workroom and studios to Fulham in September 1985. They celebrated the tenth birthday of the company with the Barnardo's gala evening attended by its president, HRH The Princess of Wales. By now the Bruce Oldfield name was internationally recognised.

For Bruce, the partnership with Anita is invaluable.

'We've been together through thick and thin, and she's my best friend. There is an endemic *folie de grandeur* in this business, but there is nothing like that with Anita. I've seen many partnerships, but I've yet to meet anybody who's such a great all-rounder. On a day-to-day business level, she's very easy-going, but she's also tough – nobody tries to pull the wool over Anita's eyes. In the past she's been a jack of all trades and worked ceaselessly with me to build up the business. I have an absolute faith in her business sense, because she frees me to concentrate on design and promotional activities. In the final reckoning, she is a unique business woman.' Anita sees their relationship as 'a strong partnership. To some degree, our personalities have merged over the years, and I feel that we are usually aware of each other's thoughts. Although I look after the business side, he will often suggest avenues to be explored, whilst also accepting my occasional, constructive criticism on collections. I think it of paramount importance that he should focus on design.' What advice does she have to give to young designers starting out today? 'The business environment has changed enormously in fashion since 1975. It's become far more professional. I think it imperative for one partner to have a minimum of, say, five years' business experience, to have a knowledge of the pitfalls and the sudden hypes of this business. Without that valuable experience, I think success would be short-lived.'

JOB: to oversee the expansion of the company and the wider recognition of the Bruce Oldfield name. To ensure that all aspects of the business are running smoothly, both from the point of view of the staff and the customer. To iron out over- and under-staffing, to deal with work relations. To oversee licensing contracts, check importation problems, deal with agents, buyers and some aspects of press co-operation. To make certain that orders don't get cancelled because deliveries aren't running to schedule.

Georgina Alexander-Sinclair,
personal assistant to Bruce Oldfield

Started working with clothes as a shop assistant at Brother Sun in the King's Road, and went on to be a junior sales assistant to Belville Sassoon: 'I wanted to be working closer to the centre of things, and in a smaller and younger company.' She joined Bruce Oldfield in 1980, first as Anita's assistant, and later, developing her own areas of responsibility, as Bruce's.

JOB: to organise Bruce's life to run as smoothly as possible. To anticipate and iron out problems. To attend meetings with

Bruce or on his behalf. To liaise with Anita on projects and undertake research. To answer invitations, stand in for Bruce whenever possible, arrange his trips, co-ordinate between him and the workroom, deal with customers' orders. At collection time, to work closely with the producer over rehearsals, dress allocation, running orders, styling, and organisation of accessories. To oversee the styling of Bruce Oldfield clothes used in other shows. To have a working knowledge of the latest models and find models at short notice for TV or press interviews. To set up Bruce Oldfield shoots. To buy in accessories for the shop, look for new sources, and generally keep an eye on developments in the fashion world.

Christine Fox,
production manager
Joined Bruce Oldfield through the Topstitch Agency in 1982. She studied at the London College of Fashion for a two-year technical pattern cutting course in light clothing, and spent one year as a junior assistant pattern cutter in evening and cocktail wear for Tina Warren.
At Clifton Slimline, a mail-order outsize wear company, she worked as pattern cutter for four years, precision cutting for multiples of thousands. Christine worked a day's trial for Bruce Oldfield, cutting a toile from a sketch, and making a paper pattern from the toile (a toile is a prototype garment made in a cheap version of the intended fabric – usually cotton mull or calico, sometimes lining fabric for dresses intended to be made in silk or satin). She became pro-duction manager after three years with the company.
JOB: to supply orders to buyers and to make sure the shop is fully stocked. To trial, select and employ outworkers. To record finished garments and store them in the stockroom ready to be invoiced, freighted and sent by assistants Katie Letman and Serena Morton. The production manager is also responsible for the following:
Two *order books*, one for wholesale, one for private clients. Clients' orders are entered in columns – order, garment style (e.g. coat-dress), pattern number, quantity, sizes, fabric, colour and unit cost, the cost to the buyer per garment wholesale. (The *stocking-in book*, which logs the receipt of the fabrics, is kept by the stock manager.)
Docket book. When an outworker is given a dress to make up, the docket book is used to record the order in triplicate, with copies for the auditor, the outworker, and the production manager's records.
Costing book. The costing sheets are clipped into this book one by one as each

pattern reaches the sample stage. These sheets bear a sketch with the style number and cloth and lining details, widths and costs. On very expensive items such as private clients' wedding dresses, they also record the time taken for tacking, machining, specialist work and finishing.

Judith Wolkenfeld,
workroom manager and Bruce Oldfield's 'right hand'

Studied pattern-making and design at the Barrett Street Technical College, her course funded by the Czech Committee (Judith's family had escaped from Czechoslovakia in 1938). She completed her studies in record time and went to work for Lisscraft Sportswear Ltd. In 1966 she met Anita Richardson, then a twenty-one-year-old production assistant at Angela Gore. Judith and her husband Felix ran their own company, producing the clothes for Anita at

Tsaritsar, and making up Bruce Oldfield's first independent collection. She has been with Bruce for eleven years. 'We have a great bond. We have both decided that the past is not going to hold us back.'
JOB: to 'translate Bruce's fantasy into reality.' To run the workroom with its nine machinists, five juniors and four pattern cutters, planning ahead so that everyone is fully occupied day by day. To act as mediator between designer and pattern cutter when turning sketches into toiles. To ensure fine workmanship and sort out any problems that may occur with the dozen garments that, at any one time, are passing through the workroom simultaneously. To keep up to schedule with main production as well as private fittings. 'Nothing is older to Bruce than yesterday's sketch. He wants to start working up a design *now*.' To keep Bruce, Anita, George and Christine informed about

progress without stopping for a meeting, and to sort out any problems in the workroom, from bickering to family sickness.

Lynne Sollit,
pattern cutter

Took the two-year pattern cutting course in light clothing at the London College of Fashion, and worked for three years in Bond Street in the workroom of Japanese evening-wear designer Hachi. In 1984 she went to Bruce Oldfield to cut sample patterns. While the workroom expands and contracts seasonally, Lynne remains to cut the private customers' orders, particularly for wedding dresses.
JOB: to translate Bruce's sketches into toiles and paper patterns for production. The toile fabric is cut flat on the cutting table, or may be draped, pinned and cut on to a dummy stand. As each piece of cloth is cut it is precisely copied in brown

paper. The paper pieces come together into the pattern. The cloth is machined together into the finished toile, shown to Bruce for approval and adjusted if necessary, each adjustment being copied on to the paper pattern. The pattern is given a style number, and sent downstairs for cutting into the intended fabric; the toile remains for the machinist to use for reference when she receives the completed kit to make up.

Lindy Gibbon and Eris Cross,
sample cutters

Lindy came to the company through the Topstitch Agency at a time when Bruce Oldfield was expanding and opening the shop. Born in Granada and living in London, she took the two-year course in manufacturing design at Chiswick Polytechnic before training for one year at Frank Usher, and working for Nettie Vogues for six years. Eris came to England from Trinidad in 1964, and worked for a number of companies, including Yuki. She came to work for Bruce Oldfield in 1983. In accordance with Oldfield policy, both were asked to 'trial' before being offered a job. They came in to cut out jersey dresses from paper patterns. The dresses were made up, found to be accurately cut, and both were taken into the company.

JOB: to cut the samples from the brown paper patterns supplied by the pattern cutter, and to make up the 'kits' for the workroom. These polythene bags contain the cut pieces of fabric with all the trimmings, buttons, and finishings required for the machinist to put together a complete garment, working from the finished sample.

Emilia Espinosa,
machinist

Born in Cadiz, she learnt dressmaking from the age of six, like many Spanish and Portuguese women in the industry. She came to London after the closure of the border with Gibraltar in 1971. An outworker for Tsaritsar, she became a founder member of the Bruce Oldfield company when she joined Bruce and Anita as a machinist in 1975. She witnessed every fluctuation in the company's early fortunes, and is the machinist whose wages Bruce could only pay on one occasion by selling a lamp.

JOB: to make up the garments from toile to finished outfit. To use her exceptional technical skill with every kind of fabric from fur to chiffon to carry out designs which are particularly demanding: to make up the most important commissions.

Marie Todd and Neila Souissi,
co-manageresses of the Bruce Oldfield shop

Both have worked in the shop since it opened in

June 1984. From Durham, Marie had already worked in a designer shop in Kensington when she came to Bruce and Anita by personal recommendation. Neila, from Tunisia, had met Bruce when she sold him shirts and ties in her previous job at Ashley & Blake, also in Beauchamp Place. She finds her command of three languages extremely useful in dealing with Bruce Oldfield's international customers.

Both have a greater than usual knowledge of their customers' tastes and preferences, keeping a detailed card index on each client. Consequently their suggestions and advice are valued by the customers. Occasionally Marie or Neila will make the choice for them and send the dress by post. JOB: to sell the clothes. To advise, suggest and alert the customer when new stock arrives. To keep each client's name, address and telephone number for invitations to the private customers' shows. To send out Christmas cards. To keep sales records for the accountant in the invoice book, adding up each day's takings before banking, so that Bruce or Anita can review the season financially and compare sales month for month with the previous year.

Mike and Lucy Shlafer,
US agents

Founded their agency, M. Shlafer Associates Incorporated, in 1976. Lucy had previously run her own interior design business: Mike had worked in corporate marketing. In 1978 Horizon Associates was formed to handle the import and distribution side of the business. The two sides of the agency, says Mike, 'go beyond normal agency services. We co-ordinate our clients' PR, trade publicity, and advertising and promotions publicity with American stores, as well as providing other fashion agent services.' They first took on the Bruce Oldfield account in 1985.

JOB: to handle the profile of the Bruce Oldfield collection in the USA, both with the press and in the retail market. To ensure that the important US newspaper and magazine staff attend the Oldfield collection in London by contacting them in advance, making sure the Oldfield identity and standing are known to them, and passing on their London addresses and telephone numbers to Anita Richardson so that the invitations are waiting when they arrive in England. In the retail field, to take orders for the clothes from the US, to check the credit-worthiness of the companies, and to act as contact in case of any problems from either the UK or the US. To ensure that no Oldfield clothes are diverted into the many cut-price boutiques or discount stores across the country, and that they are sold at the correct price. To come to London at collection times so that Bruce Oldfield can take them through the collection point by point, show them what goes with what, and so that they can meet, check out and take orders from the US buyers who decide to place their orders straight away. To supply Bruce Oldfield with feedback in terms of American reactions, and to advise him on such matters as the US climate and suitable fabric for resort wear.

Margaret Carter,
accountant

Having learnt book-keeping before she left school, she joined an accountancy firm, Price Waterhouse, before coming to the Bruce Oldfield company in October 1985 through an accountancy personnel agency. She enjoys the humour and informality of the fashion atmosphere.

JOB: to keep the records, mark the cash flow, deal with the wages and insurance. To sort out staff problems. To pay the fabric suppliers. An important part of her job recently has been to work on the viability of special projects for Bruce Oldfield: for instance, to assess the cash flow and the new revenue from licensing in order to see whether the company would be well advised to open a bigger shop in London or a first shop in New York, and if so whether they should wait one or two years before doing so.

Rosalind Woolfson of Shandwick Communications,
press representative

Worked in the press office of Marks & Spencer for several years before moving into PR consultancy and handling, amongst other accounts, the UK launch of McDonalds. In 1975 Ros joined Shandwick (now

the largest PR group in the country), and has worked for a very wide range of clients, including hosiery and lingerie manufacturers Charnos. She has overall responsibility for the promotion of silk in the UK, and she runs the press office for various exhibitions, notably the British Designer Shows held twice a year at Olympia. When the Bruce Oldfield shop opened in 1984, Anita rang to ask if Ros would work for them. 'Because Shandwick are a major public relations group, Ros has bigger horizons than most fashion PRs,' Anita says. 'Ros is extremely professional: the best. She knows everything about fashion and PR.' Ros is now a director of Shandwick Com-munications, a sub-sidiary of Shandwick plc, where she heads the company's fashion, arts and design section. Ros handles Bruce's publicity selectively. 'This is fundamental.

There are many people who ring up and want me to arrange something with Bruce, and I ensure that everyone receives an answer. But at that time, it may not be appropriate for Bruce to appear on that programme, or in that publication, because it will not advance his interests, it will make unnecessary demands on his energy, or it could have an adverse effect. For example, people want to talk to him about what he's made for the Princess of Wales on one of her state visits abroad. We don't talk about *any* private client. But more than that, if details were allowed out it could backfire if the clothes aren't worn, which happens. And most importantly, we would not do anything to jeopardise Bruce's relations with the Palace. My work is founded on instinct, experience and an understanding of what Bruce is trying to achieve; and I organise his public profile.'

On their working relationship: 'I believe strongly in Bruce's work and I feel privileged to be part of it. He is an excellent media man. He knows how to relax in front of the cameras, how to behave for them, and how to enjoy it. Sometimes we joke that I'm Bruce's minder.'
Under her care, Bruce has become enough of a celebrity to appear on Radio 4's *Desert Island Discs*, and in a feature on British Fashion Week for the BBC's *Nine O'Clock News*, with its guaranteed maximum exposure.
Ros introduced Charnos and Bruce Oldfield to each other, which resulted in the hosiery licensing deal. She also arranged a dinner party for another client at which she introduced Bruce to Karl Lagerfeld – 'That's the sort of thing that increases his international profile.'
JOB: to forward Bruce Oldfield's best interests in terms of media coverage internationally. To promote him in

productive areas and maintain discretion over other matters. To invite the foreign press to the showing of the collection and keep them fully informed, and to organise the seating plan from a working knowledge of the publications and personalities involved. To have a grasp of the controlling business interests concerned in the international fashion world, in order to make connections advantageous to the company.

NOT FORGETTING TAILOR

A
SEASON
ENDS

4

A
SEASON
BEGINS

OCTOBER
Bath and Frankfurt

It is 29 October, the first day of the Interstoff fabrics fair and traditionally the day the fashion business arrives in Frankfurt *en masse* and fixes its sights on the winter collections for the following year. Bruce Oldfield, however, has a prior engagement in Bath. Now, at 7.30 a.m., he is reading *The Times* folded back to Suzy Menkes' fashion page:
'I chose Bruce Oldfield's elegant evening outfit as Dress of the Year to go on permanent display as the fashion imprint of 1985 at the Museum of Costume in Bath . . . for his skills as a dressmaker, for his belief in cut, line and silhouette, for his standards of workmanship and for his conception of women.'
The column goes on to mention every triumph that has made 1985 Bruce Oldfield's year – the gala fashion show in aid of Dr Barnardo's, attended by HRH The Princess of Wales in one of her Oldfield dresses, record sales in the Beauchamp Place shop, the new premises in Fulham and the agreements to design furs and hosiery. Bruce is on his way to Bath for the presentation of the dress to the Costume Museum, driving on to Heathrow afterwards to arrive in Frankfurt by early evening. He is picked up by Ros Woolfson, his press representative at Shandwick Communications, who mentions on the way to the car that she was contacted the previous day by the *Daily Mirror*.
'They wanted to borrow six of your samples, then asked if the Princess of Wales had taken any of them with her to Australia. I knew what they were up to. I told them that most unfortunately every single one of your samples was abroad.'
By 11.30 a.m. Bruce Oldfield is drinking champagne in the octagonal room of the Bath Museum. With him stand Scott Crolla, the menswear designer, uneasily conscious of his title for today, 'Peacock Male of 1985'; and Kevin Arpino of Adele Rootstein who contributed the fibreglass mannikins already wearing the Oldfield dress and a Crolla outfit downstairs. Curator Penelope Byrd leads up a young girl with a tape recorder who wishes to ask Bruce some questions for Great Western Radio. She is the only member of the press present. Bruce's eyes meet Ros' over her head and, thinking of the spot they had to turn down to be here today, the invisible bubble between them reads 'And we could have had *TV AM*!' But Bruce walks with the reporter to a quiet corner, where he obligingly gives her all the information she needs.
The room is filling up with people. Behind the scenes Bruce's Brazilian-born model Rio is already zipped into the presentation dress and putting the final touches to her make-up. Anita Richardson, Bruce's partner, business organiser and friend, joins the group, blonde and smiling. Suzy Menkes, in a black velvet Chanel suit, leads up His Worship the Mayor, surprisingly a stalwart lady in mayoral chain and substantial green Windsmoor suiting who explains that she is fitting in the Costume Museum between a civic reception for the International Volleyball Confederation and a dinner for the Gas Federation.
Suzy Menkes climbs on to the rostrum, is briefly introduced by Mr Mayor, and in her turn introduces Bruce, and then the Dress of the Year. Rio glides in on cue and circles the room between the crowd: there are murmurs of admiration for the dress, a curve of gilded pleating cut into a bias furl of black silk. Mr Mayor, with some hesitation, gives her verdict.
'Jolly nice dress. Quite practical, too. You could really stride out with that split skirt.'

NICK BRIGGS/*THE TIMES*

'Look on the bright side,' whispers Anita in Bruce's ear. 'We can't be long over lunch. The car will be waiting and we have to leave here at 3 to get the plane at 5.30.'

At 9 a.m. the next morning, Frankfurt looks like the most depressing place in the world. The greasy modern streets are smeared with cold rain and packed with rush-hour traffic. The majority of the people assembled early in the entrance to Interstoff could be waiting to go in to a Conservative Party Conference, so remote do they look from fashionable pursuits.

The biggest international fabric preview in the world, it is held bi-annually and kicks off each new fashion season, enabling designers and trend-spotters from all over the world to see wholesale manufacturers from different countries display their new fabrics in one place. The winter collections start here, on six floors of two gigantic halls in the Messe, the Olympia of West Germany. This, the eighteenth exhibition of the year, is sandwiched between the publishing world's annual Book Fair and an office equipment show.

The forthcoming winter collection show will be a particularly important event for Bruce Oldfield. It is his first ready-to-wear show after four years of concentrating on couture. Frankfurt will supply the fabrics to be shown on the catwalk – prototypes of the garments he will sell in his shop, the boutique in Harvey Nichols and all over the world through big international stores and fashion boutiques. He has to balance the plains and the prints which will mix and match and lead customers on from blouse to skirt to jacket. He needs show-stoppers and simple jersey fabrics, both the glitz and the bread and butter. He is not only buying for the ready-to-wear collection but for his private clients, for whom he runs a made-to-measure couture service. He knows from long experience that the fabric companies will be pressuring him to buy in 'pieces' – lengths of thirty-five to forty metres – whereas he only needs between five and ten metres for sampling. When the orders come in, he will follow up with bigger orders for stock.

Bruce Oldfield ready-to-wear prices run from £300 to £2,000. His exclusive made-to-measure dresses cost from £2,000 to £5,000, with wedding dresses up to £20,000. 'Wedding guest is about as "day" as we get,' he says.

It is his ninth Interstoff. He leads the way along aisles of booths, each one bursting with flowers and beaming cloth merchants presiding over an average of 750 samples for each company.

Bruce goes to one end of the rail, Anita to the other. They work towards each other and cross over to cover the ground twice.

'The most difficult thing to find is a good plain you can make into a blouse, a jacket, a pair of trousers,' Bruce says, 'something you can wear to a restaurant, a theatre and on afterwards . . . that's the way you have to think. This one's nice.'

'Yes,' says Anita. 'Nice for the craft shop in Coventry.'

'At the end of the day the onus is on me,' Bruce says to the salesman. 'If Madame here doesn't like it, I'll still get it.'

At Corisia, a large Italian company, Bruce gets a big welcome. In a business where continuity impresses more than money they have been selling to him for four years.

Anita picks out a glossy grey jacquard. 'Mmm.'

Bruce comes over, feels it, 'Mmm.'

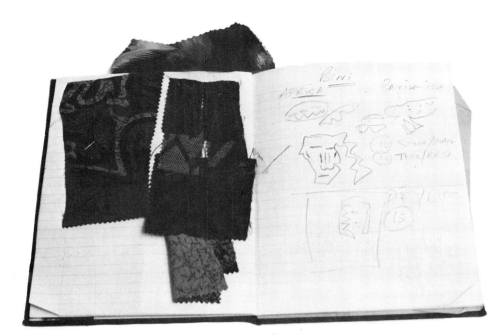

THE NOTEBOOK,
WITH CUTTINGS OF
SAMPLES BOUGHT

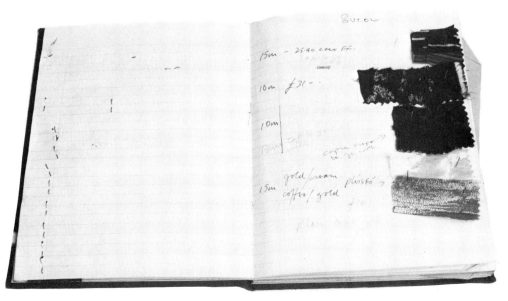

'JUST HOW MANY YUKKY
GREENS DO WE ALREADY
HAVE?'

BRUCE AND ANITA WORK
FROM OPPOSITE ENDS OF
THE RACK

He pulls out three or four bronze-coloured samples and puts them on top of the rack. 'That's interesting. What the hell is it?' The fabric is part woven, part printed, and looks as if someone has painted chocolate roses with Christmas-tree glitter. He reads the label. 'Cotton and acetate.'

He squints over a cigarette, standing hunched over the rail, frowning. He is offered his first glass of champagne. It is 10.15.

With an armful of samples, Bruce and Anita move to a glass-topped table, sit down and get out the calculator. Anita indicates the ticket of a fine cashmere. 'We're pushing our luck with this, aren't we?'

'Yeah,' says Bruce. 'At that price, who would you trust to make it? A wool suit in the shop's £1,000, so cashmere would be . . .'

The appeal of the fabric fails to outweigh the cost, and the cashmere joins the rejects.

'The good thing about this firm', Anita says, 'is that they do different weights in the same colours, so you can pick out two fabrics that will really match.'

Giuseppe Pedroletto comes over to clarify the pricing. He has been six years with the company and has just returned from showing the fabrics in the USA for three weeks. He looks, and is, a tired man.

'Local Italian price?' Bruce asks, indicating a jersey.

'We still have to add on delivery.'

'Polyester in it?'

'It's ribboned into the fabric.'

'We'll point that out to our customers.' Anita says, laughing. 'It'll help to explain the price!'

'It's not bad,' says Bruce. 'We'll be buying this, but not today. I have to work out the colours first, see some more companies. You'll give me ten-metre lengths?'

It turns out that this request is not possible: the material is piece-dyed, a whole piece at a time, and thus a length taken from one piece may not match exactly the colour of a length taken from another. S. Pedroletto, however, assures Bruce that he can have whatever lengths he likes from the other fabrics. Then he picks up a silver spot and drops it in front of Bruce. 'Jacques Azagury chose this one.'

'Then I don't want it, do I?' Exclusivity is vitally important at the Oldfield/Azagury end of the market. Some manufacturers keep exclusivity lists, others do not. The previous year, Armani, Dior and Krizia, plus a few designers in London, all ordered the same fabric from one manufacturer. But any manufacturer who allows this to happen could run the risk of alienating the designers.

Bruce is wringing a sample in his hands. 'There's something wrong with this one. It's too limp. £110 a metre? For that price, I want diamonds on it!' Still, he is fascinated by it. He looks over to Anita. 'This has that

AT INTERSTOFF, YOU CAN
COMPARE, ASK QUESTIONS
OF THE MANUFACTURERS
THEMSELVES AND CHECK
OUT EXCLUSIVITY

kind of dingy Italian chic. What do you think?'
'I think it's dingy,' says Anita. 'Why not this lime silky one?'
'I'll show you why not.' He reverses the fabric, rubs the palm of his hand over it and shows how cobwebby threads spring up over the surface. He turns back one last time to the other fabric. 'I'm drawn to this chic dingy Italian thing – but you've got to remember it looks great on that skin with that sun. Put it with a northern European skin on a grey January day . . . forget it!'

In a small, crowded stall on lane B, Bruce shows Anita a flocked silk. 'Just watch what this does on the bias.' He pulls gently, and blisters appear all over the surface. 'Like cellulite!' says Anita. She pulls out a lumpy fabric in cerise, orange and chocolate. 'Is this what you're looking for? It's a bit as if someone's been sick!'
'On the other hand,' says Bruce, indicating another silk, 'this one's fab. And dressy blouses is an area we could have done with this year.'

When it comes down to price, there are various calculations to be made. Bruce wants from this manufacturer ten metres of a pure silk print of cherubs and roses. The salesman wants him to buy half a piece, and adds, 'If you go under eighteen metres we put on a twenty per cent surcharge.'

Bruce asks whether the quoted price is 'FOB' (Freight On Board, or delivery as far as the border of its country of origin), or CIF (Carriage, Insurance, Freight). Although the Common Market countries pay no duty between them, all being members of the European Free Trade Association, careful pricing is vital, taking into account all possible extra charges. The price agreed will eventually be set at the exchange rate when the fabric comes in, and that price is adhered to for the rest of the season. The prices Bruce and Anita are working out are only a guide to the final cost. To the quoted price of a fabric Bruce adds the company's standard nine per cent for carriage and five per cent to cover currency fluctuations. The fabrics he has ordered by the end of the morning work out at £17, £14.20, £17.70 and £18.90 a metre. He hesitates over the last one. 'That's expensive.'

A pattern is emerging in the notebook where he staples the tiny cuttings Anita takes from the samples he's buying. There are tobacco bronzes and limey greens, blacks and whites with dull silver, scarlets and dark greens. He squints over 225 shades of crêpe de chine, flicking over eight tones of olive. 'That's cool.'

'Just how many yukky greens do we already have?' Anita asks. Working from opposite ends of a rack they both simultaneously pull out a black and white newspaper print Lurex rose.

They pass by a manufacturer with Yves Saint Laurent links. 'Everything,' says Bruce, 'ends up looking too YSL.'

By 1.45 Bruce has spent around £4,000. Lunch is eaten in the Hall Four ground-floor restaurant with British designers met along the way – Rifat Ozbek, Jacques Azagury, Ninivah Khomo, and her husband Zak. Everyone is at Interstoff to choose fabrics, and running into other designers making their selections can be embarrassing. But there's a code of honour to be observed: you look the other way. Over lunch, everyone is relaxed. They choose, with expressions of disgust, between ox muzzle salad, brawn and veal balls. 'They eat the strangest parts of animals here!'

At 4.30, after seeing several more manufacturers,

Bruce is almost ready to call it a day. Michel Guigou of Bucol, a Christian Dior lookalike and a third generation textile manufacturer, knows Bruce's work and the names of his most famous customers. When Bruce asks if he can buy in ten-metre quantities, M. Guigou is happy to accommodate him. 'You can have whatever you want.'

Quick to press home an advantage, Bruce asks, 'Eight metres?'

'Anything.'

'By next Wednesday? I've promised a dress for a certain ambassador's wife.'

'Sure.'

They come out of Bucol at 5.15 p.m. and Bruce has spent £8,500. Like everyone they pass, Bruce and Anita have threads hanging from their jackets, and the floor sparkles with dropped sequins and glitter fall-out.

It is 9.30 a.m. the next day, and Bruce and Anita want to catch a mid-afternoon flight out of Frankfurt. At Corisia they hunch over the jersey samples again, unable to decide.

'Are you sure you're not going to hate these when they come in?' Anita asks.

'Quite possibly.'

'Whenever we deliberate too long we never use the fabrics.'

The peeved look leaves Bruce's face. He sits back and says 'OK. We'll choose these from the rep in London.' The advantage of choosing fabrics at Interstoff is that you can compare, ask questions of the manufacturers themselves and check out exclusivity. These factors are not so important when choosing a basic cloth that a designer will run every season.

S. Pedroletto has the answer to a query Bruce has about printed jersey.

'We are saying we'll discharge on jersey for you,' he tells Bruce, indicating a willingness on Corisia's behalf to print a piece specially to Bruce's requirements.

'Great!'

'Will you come to Milan and visit us? Then you can choose exactly what you want.'

Bruce knows the advantages that a special relationship can bring between a top fabric house and a designer. He says he will go.

'Now,' says Bruce, looking at his watch, 'let's look for a bit of flash.'

At Etro, fabrics and shapes begin to coalesce in Bruce's mind. He makes a few sketches in his notebooks. They haven't done business here before. The salesman's eyes flicker curiously from Bruce to Anita.

'I want to buy prints,' Bruce tells her, looking up from the sketchbook. 'Why do we never do prints in winter? Explain it to me.'

'Because you don't like prints, Bruce. You're not a print person.'

'Until I see a print I like.'

He picks out some vivid African prints depicting masks, cave paintings and animals: these are the cause of their first real disagreement.

'I just think they're just too big to wear,' says Anita.

'And I think they are kind of light for winter.'

'They don't *look* light. I think it's the alternative to beading and glitter, because they are bright and strong. And they'll sell well in the summer, in the shop in August.' He buys a couple of short lengths for samples.

On the ground floor Bruce looks in a desultory way at zips and buttons. But the booths are already emptying on this final day of the Fair. Samples are beginning to be packed away early, and knots of people stand in the aisles talking about times of planes. Bruce and Anita have spent over £10,000. They have achieved more or less all they set out to do, buying in lengths for samples, covering the prints – although not all the plains – and choosing almost all of the likely show-stoppers. The clippings, all together in Bruce's notebook, show a sense of co-ordination and discipline that bodes well for the mix and match elements in the collection. They are reasonably pleased. They collect their luggage from the lockers and head for the taxi rank.

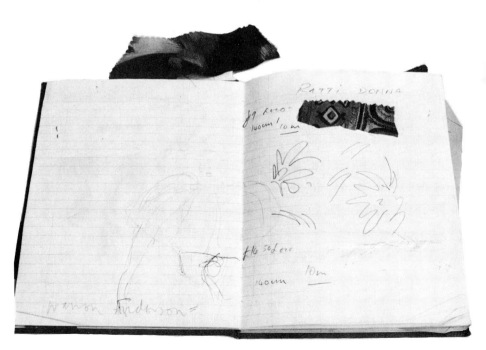

5

DESIGN: *House Style*

Designing is a continuous process, and it goes on whether or not I am putting together a collection. I'm prolific! Ideas arrive from everywhere – a jacket turned inside out, a piece of cloth that has fallen on to the floor. Or I might become interested in, say, Edwardian clothes, in which case I'll go to a museum and do some research.

Wherever you find inspiration, it is no good unless you take it further. You have to recognise it, develop it, and then perhaps apply it in another way. Developing an idea from the initial stimulus through to the finished garment can be as lengthy a process as you wish to make it. You can completely lose sight of the initial thought and go on to a quite different theme, but the original idea has been entered into the 'computer' by then and you find it becomes part of your mental reference library. The developing process becomes an almost mechanical formula of trial and error. You add, you subtract, you change the context. I like to see how the material works at the same time as I'm making sketches. I go backwards and forwards between stand and drawing board. I'll be working on a dressmaking technique such as smocking, pleating or ruching, pinning it on the stand, sewing a bit. Then having seen and understood what the fabric is doing, I'll start drawing as many permutations as possible around the idea. It looks good on the shoulder of that dress, how would it be on the hip? Instead of a limp, draping kind of cloth, how would it look in taffeta or another stiff fabric? Draw it, pin it in taffeta, develop it. Discard it if it doesn't please me. Then consider the colour. What would the

difficult to sit down?

Based on Boned bodice

Swags in velvet. crin to hold wings out

satin in Jersey

'SCULPTURED' EVENING DRESSES

TRANSLATING SKETCH
INTO REALITY: 'YOU CAN
SIT AND DRAW UNTIL THE
COWS COME HOME, BUT
UNLESS YOU CAN TRANS-
LATE THAT INTO A DRESS
ON A CUSTOMER'S BACK
IT DOESN'T MEAN A
THING'

introduction of a contrast colour do for it? Back to the drawing board.

It is a discipline that anyone could use, but another designer, starting from the same original stimulus and following a similar process, would end up with a totally different garment. His view of the way the end product should ideally look, moulded by his personal concept of style, is going to be different from mine. When I'm asked to define the Bruce Oldfield style, I often say I don't know yet. By which I mean I never want to get to the point where you are turning out the look that everyone expects of you, season after season. What the press usually say about my clothes is that they are sexy. If I analyse that I come back to the core of whatever philosophy I have about putting cloth around a woman. I think of the female form as a series of curves, and the rhythm of these curves and proportions is something you can use whether you are designing a dress, a shoe, or a pair of sunglasses. I envisage garments in the round, and if I'm working with a detail I will always be watching to see how that detail can move around the body. So spirals of ruching, embroidered seams, whatever the theme, it takes on a sensual line. Because I think in the round, when I'm designing I'm not just bending over a desk all day. I'm sketching, jumping up to pin a length of cloth on the stand, doing another drawing and adjusting the cloth again, in a continuous process. You can sit and draw until the cows come home, but unless you can translate that into a dress on a customer's back it doesn't mean a thing.

At art schools all over the country you see wonderful drawings and little feeling for how to put it together. The proof of that comes when you go to the diploma shows and you notice a two-dimensional look to the

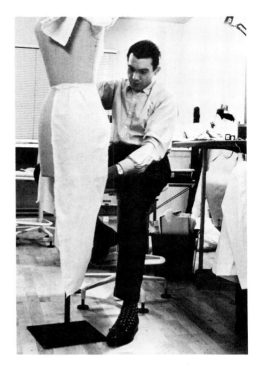

IN THE STUDIO: 'I THINK
OF THE FEMALE FORM AS
A SERIES OF CURVES . . .
I ENVISAGE DESIGNING
IN THE ROUND'

'I WORK WITH SHAPE AND FABRIC JUST AS
MUCH AS I DO WITH PENCIL AND PAPER'

clothes on the runway. If you take the students'
sketchbooks and flip through them you'll see lots of
garments drawn from the front, some from the back
and none from the side. It's not their fault that they
don't think in three dimensions, because often the
teaching tells them to make a garment that is exactly like
the drawing.

They are missing out on the vital part where you look
at the body, take some cloth and start pinning. So
what happens is that they come up with huge broad
shoulders and five-inch square pockets and a front
and back that don't flow into each other, and none of it
has anything to do with the body inside. OK, it's too
expensive for each student to have a house model – ours
cost £25 per hour – but they could be shown that the
side view is just as important to the dress as the front
view. Because I work with shape and fabric just as much
as I do with pencil and paper, ninety-eight per cent of
what I draw can be made. I hand over the sketch to the
pattern cutter with a rough-up on the stand and say
'I've proved this is feasible. Now do the technical
work'.

I have a kind of architect/draughtsman relationship
with the pattern cutter. I'm important in conceiving
the idea and making a three-dimensional mock-up.
Then I take a break while the pattern cutter takes over.
My role is important again when we get to the fittings.
This is where we put the toile on the house model and
I can see how closely the pattern cutter has interpreted
my original concept.

Fittings and refittings are all about getting the garment
right. There will be at least four of us present: myself,
the pattern cutter, the house model, and Judith
Wolkenfeld, because being in charge of the

THE FITTING: 'I'LL SUSS
OUT WHERE SOMETHING
ISN'T QUITE RIGHT OR
WHERE THE PROPORTION
HAS CHANGED'

workroom she sees the job from the machinist's point
of view and how the job should be tackled, stage by stage.
She's also a very good fitter and technician who can see
how to make adjustments and put things right.
I'll suss out where something isn't quite right or where
the proportion has been changed. Then I will be thinking
of the dress from the wearer's point of view – is it
comfortable? Can she walk, can she sit? Is it immodest? I
get a rapport going with our house model, Jane, and
encourage her to say if the dress feels tight under the
arms, or if something feels insecure. Every adjustment
to the toile will be recorded on the paper pattern. If there
are particular technical problems we call in the
machinist. Her skill lies in sewing together the jigsaw
pieces and executing the design exactly the way the
pattern cutter has intended.
Initially I'll be thinking in general fabric terms and I
will pick the cloth later, or sometimes I design a dress for
a particular piece of cloth. Either way, we get the toile
absolutely right first, because you only start cutting
into expensive cloth when you are totally confident.
Sometimes, if we are in a frantic rush to turn out a ball
dress for a particular customer, we might go straight
from the first toile fitting into the proper fabric. The
cutter will then allow for later adjustments by cutting
extra fabric in. Essentially, if the toile looks right, so
will the garment, and all the people I have mentioned are
enormously important in the process.
So much of what is called 'style' and 'luxury' comes
down to these technical processes, and the care with
which they are done. But there is an absolutely basic
and crucial reality behind the style of any fashion
house, and it is what customers are really talking about
when they say, 'Armani's trousers are fabulous on me,

but I just can't wear Saint Laurent's', or 'Calvin Klein skirts always look good on me'. It's not so much to do with sizing as proportion, and it all goes back to blocks. Every house throughout the world has developed their own blocks, and the blocks are the heart of house style. A block is a collection of pieces of brown paper pattern that act as a sort of archetype for all the clothes the house makes.

If you wanted to be an industrial spy in the fashion business you would steal the blocks, because they record in size 10 or 12 all the information relating to the way that house cuts. For Chanel, for instance, the usual shoulder line might be 11.5 centimetres, and the drop from the end of the shoulder to underarm in a set-in sleeve could be 15 centimetres. The neckline is cut ½ centimetre lower than the collar bone in front, and so on. So the block is the bible of the fashion house, the shape of the woman that Chanel want to project, the shape which flatters and has been proven over the years to suit the customer. That's the way each house has developed its system of making clothes to standard sizes, always getting the kind of look, fit and proportion the designer wants. This is the skeleton of the garment, which will change only minutely season by season. You don't decide on a block in the first year of business. You develop it as you develop your style, and it becomes your 'handwriting'.

The sizing begins from the block. If you are making for a private customer who is, say, half way between a 10 and a 12 you will take a 10 block and upgrade or a 12 block and downgrade. A size 10 will come in many different shapes. For instance our house model Jane is a size 10 like Marie Helvin, and they both have 37-inch hips, but one designer's size 10 skirt will fit Marie but

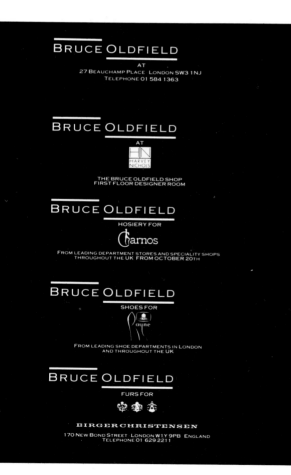

it won't fit Jane. That's because Marie has shapely hips and a flat behind, but Jane is narrow from the front with a curvy rear.

All designers have to put up with one occupational hazard. It happens when a fashion editor decides to photograph your dress in a freaky way. Some glossy borrows your serious satin dress and it appears three months later on a model with red eyes, paint-spattered hair, purple pop sox and baseball boots. So I welcome the opportunity I now have to take big runs of advertising in top magazines and show my clothes the way I see them, on the kind of woman I like to see wearing them, with the right make-up, jewellery, gloves, hats and shoes. I think that these six- and twelve-page runs in key issues of *Vogue* may do more for getting my style across and for customer awareness than even a fashion show. It's the revenue from licensing and the success of the shop that enable me to do this.

It would be wrong to discuss house style and leave out Colin Barnes' drawings for the private customers, which are an interesting part of how we present ourselves to the public. Colin Barnes is a well-known fashion artist who works here and in Paris, and I met him at Ravensbourne where he taught fashion illustration. In the old days of couture the fashion houses would employ sketchers who would come in and draw the dresses on a model, redrawing them in several different permutations of fabric. Then the client could see the sample on a model and look through a pile of drawings which would help her to choose a fabric. My own sketches are shorthand – I understand them, but a customer wouldn't. So, as a special favour to me, Colin Barnes does a portfolio of finished drawings of wedding dresses and evening dresses for the private

NEIL KIRK

customers, showing precisely what we are offering. He
draws twenty wedding dresses for each nine-month
period, and thirty evening dresses for each six-month
period.

The house style, if you take it apart and examine it
properly, is all these different elements working
together. It is the designer's talents at work, technical
mastery, the development of successful blocks,
practical and popular sizing, and the ability to project
yourself as you want.

DRAWINGS BY COLIN
BARNES: 'HOW WE
PRESENT OURSELVES
TO THE PUBLIC'

PEPLUM JACKET WITH
BEADING, LONG SKIRT

BEADED WEDDING
GOWN, BIAS CUT:
LACE SPIRALS; 'FISH-
TAIL' TRAIN

EVOLUTION
Costings

Dress PC (*for private clients*) 16.
*Crystal-leaf embroidered silk crêpe dress
with full sweeping skirts.*
Selling price: £4,300

Judith Wolkenfeld thinks that only the most experienced pattern cutters can attempt to realise some of Bruce's deceptively simple dresses. This one was difficult to get right. The pattern of the beading had to fit exactly into the pattern of the garment's body shape; every seam had to match the beadwork perfectly. In practice the dress had to be made up once in the correct fabric, taken to pieces for the beading pattern, sent off to be beaded in fresh cloth and then skilfully reassembled.

To begin, the pattern cutter cut the pattern and made a toile (the calico mock-up) of Bruce's sketch. This dress was a model to be used in couture services, rather than an individual commission, and so it was fitted on Jane, the house model. Alterations were simultaneously made to the paper pattern. Lindy, the cutter, was given a docket to cut the bodice in silk crêpe and lining. This was assembled for another fitting session to check that the pattern had been adjusted correctly. Alterations were again copied into the paper pattern. At this point, the flowing-leaf bead embroidery, which was a recurring motif in the collection, was drawn on to the paper pattern, making sure that the design moved in an unbroken line through all the many seams and darts of the fitted body. Rajinder Sahajpal, the embroiderer, then took the fabric and the pattern away for beading. Meanwhile, Lynne cut the full circular skirts using a second toile in crêpe. These could not be finished until the beaded section had been finished. Two weeks later, on the return of the beadwork, Lynne tacked together the complete bodice, matching all the seams for the embroidery design, and refitted it on Jane. There were some major adjustments, due to the fact that a fine fabric, when beaded under tension on frames, can

become distorted, and sometimes the weight of beads can elongate a bodice. This was a crucial fitting at which the fitter and seamstress needed all their skills to dovetail the different elements of the dress into a perfect entity.

Emilia was given the job of finally seaming the dress together, detailed work that took five days to complete, down to levelling and hand-sewing the enormous hems.

Besides the cost of the fabric and haberdashery, and the time and craftsmanship put into the beading, the costing has to include the labour involved in each stage of the evolution of the dress. It must take account of the time taken for cutting the first pattern, making the calico toile, fitting it with Judith, Lynne, Bruce and Jane and making the first pattern alterations, for cutting and fitting the crêpe bodice and toile with the same people. present, for the second pattern alterations, drawing up the design motif, cutting skirts and linings, and tacking the dress together for the final fitting, this time with Judith, Lynne, Bruce and Jane, joined by Emilia; and lastly for assembling the dress, including final hand-sewing and alterations to beadwork. In all, the making of the dress took one month. It is the craftsmanship and the labour-intensity that make such a dress a high-priced item.

Anita Richardson oversees all costings. 'There are also our overheads. You have to take into account the tremendous running costs of our two premises with rents, rates, sales staff, fitters and transport. Running our two bases last year cost £90,000, before wages, and we've expanded since then. Add to that the fabrics we have to keep in stock which are valued at £250,000 at any one time, the bi-annual Frankfurt buying

DRESS PC 16: TOILE FITTING

LYNNE SOLLIT ALTERS THE PAPER PATTERN

BARRY DRAWS OUT THE MOTIF

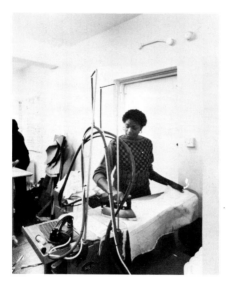

PRESSING THE BODICE PIECES

JUDITH WOLKENFELD CHECKS THE
EMBROIDERY

THE BODICE IN PROGRESS

CHECKING WHETHER THE BODICE HAS
STRETCHED

heavy beaded.

Extended shoulder with pleats sitting on shoulder pads.

3 meters of crepe Maroccain.

Velvet or crepe.

*no nets *.*

EMILIA FINISHES OFF BY HAND

PERFECTING THE DRESS

THE DRESS IN THE SHOP

trips, the fifty to sixty people we pay every month, and the cost of our fashion shows, a minimum of £25,000. After that there is the £19,000-worth of carriage and packing we need for deliveries. Even then, there's our advertising and publicity budget: last year that totalled £36,500. So what you see on the costing sheet is just the tip of the iceberg.'

Dress number 584 (ready to wear). Black jersey dress topstitched in red with a red jersey swag draping the side of the narrow skirt. Wholesale price £144. Retail price in this country: £360. The sample is being fitted on a house model and will be part of the group of jersey cocktail dresses shown together in the collection

584 was a simple and relatively quick dress to make, machine-made throughout, with only the zip put in by hand. The sketch was explicit and was translated into the toile from the basic narrow, long-sleeved dress block in the sample size 10.

As jersey stretches and falls in a completely different way from woven calico, the toile is cut in a jersey of equal quality to that of the finished garment. With dresses like this the fabric is usually taken from old stock in the previous year's colours. As the pattern cutter worked on the toile she recorded each part in a paper pattern. When the dress toile was ready it was tried on the house model and Bruce added and pinned the swag. When the paper pattern was adjusted and complete, it was cut in the intended black and scarlet jersey, put together, and tried on the house model for the second time. Judith Wolkenfeld oversaw Bruce's final adjustments and reminded the machinist to topstitch in red cotton.

Anita Richardson comments: 'We would sell this dress to our own shop and to Harvey Nichols for a wholesale price of £144. Both retailers would expect to sell the dress to the customer at around the 150 per cent mark-up, which includes VAT. Under the selling price of £360 you include what has gone into the costing – usually items such as fabric, work, buttons, labels, lining, interlining, haberdashery, shoulder pads, delivery – and what goes into the mark-up. That takes in the promotion, the shows, the carrier bags, the hangers, the advertising, the running costs. A contributory factor to the rise in retail prices over the last couple of years has been the increase in shoplifting. It's a professional crime these days, with teams working together, checking out our busy times, one of them creating a diversion while another drops a dress into their shopping basket.

'For the US price we have to add the agent's sale commission. The jersey dresses are among the cheapest in the collection, ranging from the high two-hundreds to the mid three-hundreds. As much as possible in this group is intended to be done by machine for economy's sake.'

584: 'A SIMPLE AND RELATIVELY QUICK DRESS . . .'

THE
BRUCE OLDFIELD
SHOP

27 Beauchamp Place London SW3

The shop opened in June 1984 opposite the original showroom and workroom premises, born of the need for a showplace where Bruce could have overall control of the head-to-toe look of his clothes and the way in which they were presented to clients. The ground floor shop sells the ready-to-wear collection and promotes the total Oldfield look, with jewellery and exclusive collections of hats and accessories, together with new shoes and tights made under licence. The licensing deals are expanding: soon the shop may have to be extended to accommodate a greater range of Bruce Oldfield products.

The shop's stock is chosen and bought by Neila Souissi and Marie Todd under Anita Richardson's guidance, just as if it were a separate retail outlet. Neila and Marie tailor the stock to their particular clients and the lives they lead, and are the vital link between Bruce Oldfield and the women who buy his clothes. From the first time a woman buys a garment, her sizes and preferences are noted on a card index, and her name is added to the mailing list for show invitations, Christmas cards and sales preview notices. Bruce Oldfield customers have an unusual degree of trust in the two co-manageresses, sometimes placing orders from abroad on the advice and descriptions supplied. Neila or Marie will write, sending fabric cuttings within the colour range they know the customer likes, and the customer will send a cheque or place a telephone order with a credit card. Their detailed knowledge of their customers' sizes and tastes also comes into play when they select the stock from the new collection.

It would be impossible to fit every outfit from the show into the shop, particularly when multiplied into four sizes and three or four colourways, and so the collection is edited down. Anita makes sure that within this tighter nucleus she still has a balance of jackets, skirts and pants so that the customer has a good range of alternatives. Bruce Oldfield, like many other designers, tends to show his suits without blouses on the catwalk, to emphasise the line of the jacket, whereas the customer will want something to go underneath. Anita will provide a blouse from another part of the collection, or, if necessary, ask Bruce to design a couple of extra camisoles or silk T-shirts. She also juggles the mix of fabrics – plains for jackets to go with print dresses or skirts, lighter fabrics for blouses to go with heavier cloth for pants or skirts. She memorises and checks the contents of the fabric stockroom and makes sure the cloth is used quickly, before it 'dates'. A designer tends to buy more fabric at Interstoff than he will use in the show: after all, he doesn't design the clothes until he has checked out the new fabrics available. Those that haven't been made up into samples will be utilised to stock the shop, some of them perhaps more suitable for the British climate than for the countries of the international buyers.

It is Anita's responsibility to ensure that the shop stocks the outfits that have already been photographed in the fashion editors' previews and credited to 27 Beauchamp Place. Where a certain dress or jacket has sold particularly well to the private customers in the previous season, she may decide to incorporate the ready-made version in a suitable fabric for the next season.

The autumn/winter collection shown on 15 March in Fashion Week is bought for the shop towards the end of March and starts to come through after the sales fortnight at the end of August. From then, it arrives

in weekly batches until it tails off towards the end-of-
season sale at the beginning of January.

The shop is a moveable feast, adapting to the needs of
the growing company, now an export showroom, now a
shop, now a salon. Anita has become increasingly
aware that in recent years the American buyers regard the
London show as a preview indication only, returning
to the US to assess fashion directions and budgets before
placing orders with their American agent in New York.
By the end of 1986, Bruce Oldfield has decided to
preview his next collection, spring and summer, not at
the Duke of York Barracks, but in the shop. The
collection will thus be 'at home' to foreign buyers and
press on 12 October, and will remain there for three
days, with half a dozen models standing by to show a
selection by request – either an abbreviated run-through
of key looks across the range, or particular areas such
as the jersey dresses, the late-day outfits or the ball
gowns.

Besides the preview shows for press and foreign
buyers, there are private customer shows in the shop.
In 1986 these run on 7 May for the spring and summer
collection, and on 17 September for the autumn and
winter season. The shop is emptied and closed for the
day, filled with flowers and lined with eighty little
gold chairs. On each chair is a printed card, listing the
sixty outfits by number and description, for the
customer to mark up. This show, more intimate than
the press show – the models are told to smile at the
customers and stop for them to feel the fabrics –
promotes the ready-to-wear collection but always
ends with a finale from the couture range. It runs in the
morning and the afternoon for the benefit of the 600
index- listed customers based in London.

The day after a show like this is always a very frantic one for the sales staff, who are not only putting the shop back to rights but taking the orders telephoned through by the customers. Bruce Oldfield clients enjoy an unusually personal service. Neila and Marie can usually arrange for individual requests such as a certain dress in another colour, or a matching two-piece where the jacket is needed in a size 10 and the skirt in a size 12. If a ball dress is needed at short notice, or a suit with a special hat, it can usually be managed. Before Ascot or Goodwood, motorbikes and taxis run between the shop and Argon Mews twice a day with urgent deliveries.

THE PRIVATE CUSTOMER

The made-to-measure business flourishes downstairs
at number 27, where customers have couture wedding
dresses, ball gowns and special late-day dresses made
up individually. They choose initially from a
collection of samples and fabric swatches, and return
for two or three fittings through the toile to the final
stages. The fittings are attended by Reg Knight, design
assistant, and special fitter Tina Luis, whose
workroom-cum-stockroom lies behind the fitting
room.

The couture service for private customers has been a
rewarding aspect of the Oldfield business financially,
creatively, and in terms of public profile. There were
two reasons for the decision, in 1982, to concentrate on a
strictly custom-made operation and close the doors,
for the time being, to wholesale. Bruce felt
increasingly dissatisfied with the restrictions on
quality and workmanship imposed by low price ceilings.
At the same time he did not enjoy the risks to his
company's financial stability that resulted from erratic
payments for orders from retailers who might pay late
or, in the case of the many retailers who closed down
at the end of the seventies, never.

Financially, says Anita, the decision made sense
because 'we didn't have to spend vast amounts of money
on buying fabrics in bulk in advance of the season, as
you do with wholesale. We eliminated the risks by asking
for forty per cent deposit on each commission: we still
do.'

Bruce found particular satisfaction in the response
from his clients. 'I was no longer having to deal with

MISS MASRI 'WALKS'
HER WEDDING DRESS

BRUCE AND NEILA
FIT STEFANIE POWERS

the retailers' image of the customer. I knew exactly who my clients were and I knew they wanted what I was making. I owe a great debt to some of them who have been continuously supportive – Charlotte Rampling, Joan Collins, Stefanie Powers, Bianca Jagger, Angelica Huston, Lulu, Joanna Lumley, Viscountess Astor, HRH The Duchess of Kent, and latterly, HRH The Princess of Wales. Between them, they have steered the Bruce Oldfield name into prominence.

'With the opening of the shop we were able to offer both an off-the-peg and a made-to-measure service. Once the shop was running smoothly we reintroduced our wholesale operation. All our clothes, whether sold in the shop or exported round the world, have a well-crafted, almost couture feel to them which is directly related to those years when we took the time to develop our skills in dressmaking.'

Ultimately, Bruce attaches an importance to the shop which goes beyond its value as a retail outlet, or a showplace for collections. 'In the past I have been annoyed to find shops where my clothes have been badly presented, crammed on the rails, falling off hangers. It's crucial that the clothes look fresh and untouched, particularly where you do not have a concentration of shop assistants to pick out a dress and show it to a customer. With the opening of 27 Beauchamp Place I had at last total control over how my dresses were presented and sold. The sales assistants offer a real service. They know how the clothes should be worn and they can give the customer all the advice she needs. Our display is exactly right. For me, the final result isn't a model on a catwalk, it is the woman who buys and wears the clothes. If I make her happy, that's what it is all about.'

ANGELICA HUSTON

HRH THE PRINCESS OF WALES

CHARLOTTE RAMPLING

JOAN COLLINS

STEFANIE POWERS

SUSANNE BOND, DAUGHTER
OF ALAN BOND

THE HARVEY NICHOLS BOUTIQUE

Outside the Bruce Oldfield shop in Beauchamp Place,
the only place in Britain where Oldfield clothes can
be bought is the boutique on the first floor of Harvey
Nichols, a few hundred yards away in Knightsbridge.
Ann Gowan, the sales manager on the fashion floor,
explains that the Bruce Oldfield customers in the
store are different from those in the shop. The women
who go straight to Beauchamp Place already know
the Oldfield name and may have bought dresses there
before, whereas the Harvey Nichols customer may be a
visitor encountering the designer's name for the first
time. Big-store customers may be wealthy tourists who
want to find out who the major shops are selling, or
women who do not regularly buy at that price range.
Equally, they may be Londoners who want to look at a
great many clothes before buying a dress for a special
occasion. Harvey Nichol's Designer Room buyer Paul
Davies has the Middle Eastern markets very much in
mind, as well as the wealthy European customer who
wants to compare designer with designer.
The boutique, a self-contained glass enclave on the
first floor under the Bruce Oldfield logo, has its own
shop window, counter and separate changing-room
and is set apart within a floor of the most prestigious
names in international fashion, from Karl Lagerfeld to
Jean Muir and Sonia Rykiel.

THE WINDOW DRESSER

Philip Downes, 36, began working on the retail side of the fashion industry at 20, when he took a job as a junior in a Cheltenham store and ended up as window dresser. He came to London to work on the windows for Aquascutum and then for Harvey Nichols, where in 1974 he became head window dresser. His association with Bruce Oldfield began thirteen years ago when he put the ex-student's first group of jersey dresses in the window of Wardrobe in Chiltern Street. He is responsible for several other windows in Beauchamp Place, including Kanga and Ashley Blake.

'The window of the Bruce Oldfield shop is unusual. It is tinted, which makes it rather dark in the daytime, and the view is straight through into the shop with the fitted carpet coming right up to the glass. There is only room for a couple of mannikins at the most.

'The whole point in a street like Beauchamp Place, which is crammed with small busy windows, is to have something that stands out and looks different. The fact that Bruce Oldfield dresses are unique makes it that much easier. At the moment we have one of the jersey dresses in the window, which is great because it's very graphic in scarlet and black, and has a theatrical drape that falls beautifully. It registers right across the street.

'Bruce wants his windows to look elegant, opulent and individual. As the glass is rather mysterious, shadowing the view of the interior, I make use of that to project a look that is strongly abstract and slightly wicked. Lately I've been wrapping the mannikins with gunmetal chains hung with jewels. It looks particularly fabulous at night when the lights go on inside.

'THE WHOLE POINT
IS TO HAVE SOME-
THING THAT STANDS
OUT AND LOOKS
DIFFERENT'

'BRUCE WANTS HIS
WINDOWS TO LOOK
ELEGANT, OPULENT
AND INDIVIDUAL'

'I am proud of our mannikins, which are very chic and unusual ones made by a firm called Gemini. We take the basic dummies and I then give them an exclusive look with make-up and special wigs – at the moment I have sprayed them black and gold with metallic faces, to emphasise the abstract, other-worldly look I'm aiming at.

'Normally Bruce doesn't comment on the windows, which means he's happy with them. He is very often in the shop, and I change the windows once a week, so he sees everything I do. About September I will plan a special effect for the Christmas window so we get together to discuss it, particularly if I want to add a special ingredient to the budget. Last Christmas, for instance, I gave the mannikins catlike masks in metal and broken mirror glass. They were used again when we went to Vienna to promote British fashion. Bruce took part in a gala show and had a standing exhibit, which was my responsibility. I took two tailor's dummies made in metal, and the two shop mannikins with their mirror masks, and dressed them all in toile versions of the dresses seen in the show, hooped with thick soldering wire sparkled with fragments of mirror glass.

'Occasionally opinions about the dresses that should be in the window do differ. I believe that heightened reality tempts customers into the shop, even if they then buy one of the plainer and easier dresses. So often I'd like to put a one-off sensation on the mannikin, but the ladies in the shop want to put in one of the shorter, plainer dresses because they know they can sell more of them. Very often the shop gets its own way because they do know what sells best.'

ONE DAY'S BUSINESS

Between 10 a.m. and 6 p.m. on one day towards the end of August, twenty-eight people came into the shop in Beauchamp Place, and five women bought nine dresses amounting to £7,250 in sales.

There were two ladies from the Middle East, a mother and a daughter, who bought a cocktail dress apiece; Liza Minnelli, who bought a wool crêpe jacket and skirt; the wife of a stockbroker who bought a blue silk cocktail dress and a necklace; and Jerry Hall, who came in with two teenage girls, daughters of Mick Jagger by Bianca Jagger and Marsha Hunt. She bought three dresses for herself – a cream lace and satin sheath, a short black cotton dress, and a red satin brocade evening gown – and a dress for each of the girls.

27 Beauchamp Place London SW3

8

TOWARDS

AN

EMPIRE

Licensing extends the variety of what a woman can buy that bears the designer's stamp. It will allow Bruce to expand the range of products made under his name and in his style, and makes his designs available at reachable prices to the woman who may not be able to afford one of his dresses.

If Bruce Oldfield were to start making sunglasses or shoes inside the company he would have to open new factories for their production. The obvious way to branch out into these areas is to co-operate with an established manufacturer. An agreement cannot be entered into lightly. The prospective licensee must have a name for good quality and a position in the marketplace commensurate with Bruce's own. There must be excellent sales and distribution facilities and a reputation for prompt delivery. There is a credibility factor. Retailer and customer must have confidence in a licensed product – enough to accept the tie-up between Bruce Oldfield and the shoe, the swimsuit, the tablecloth. Clearly it would be disastrous for Bruce Oldfield to be designing lampshades at this point.

Bruce and Anita have planned a five-year programme to spread the range of his design into furs, shoes, sportswear, spectacles, sunglasses, jewellery, sheets and household linen. It is hoped that 1990 will see the launch of menswear.

It is Anita Richardson who generally makes the first contact with proposed licensees, weeding out the field and then developing ideas with those in whom she recognises a future. It can take up to eighteen months to come to an arrangement. The business considerations are Anita's province, while Bruce concentrates on all aspects of the design. There are overlaps in such decisions as the suitability of a colour for tights or the positioning of a motif on a pair of stockings, when Bruce will ask for, and listen to, the opinions of Anita, George, and other members of staff. Occasionally their arguments, for or against, will override his own.

One of the design elements that interests Anita Richardson is the season's motif. 'In order to keep the continuity of different lines we need to find a motif or a design element to run through the range of collections, such as the bullion motif on the Bruce Oldfield/Rayne shoes. A motif shouldn't be overt. It has to work as an identification symbol, but the collection must have a wide appeal.

'The contract deals with areas such as royalties, minimums [guarantees of a minimum royalty in the first year], durations of contract, territories in which the goods are to be sold, the types of retail outlet, and more. Things have to be solved to the satisfaction of both sides. I refer to Bruce when a decision has to be made that requires his consent. Once a proposal is agreed in principal, it goes to our solicitor. Over the season we have been able to develop a standard licence contract which is worked and reworked to accommodate the different requirements of each project.

'Licensed goods are never treated as extraneous, separate working activities. They are an extension of the Bruce Oldfield label and thus must conform to our image of quality and style. So as well as being a reputable company, the licensee must then satisfy other criteria. He or she has to spend a minimum figure on informing both trade and consumer of the link-up with Bruce Oldfield. All publicity is closely monitored by us to ensure that it meets our approval in both style and content. As each licensee is contractually obliged to advertise to the public, we have begun serious advertising campaigns in the major glossy magazines. The idea is to present all the lines in a consolidated, cohesive manner. The image and mood of these products must be strong. Each licensee pays us a contribution to the cost of the advertisements, including such items as models, make-up, photographers, location and stylist. There are also design and art editing fees, and on top of all this there is the expense of placing the advertisements in the magazines – *Vogue*, for instance, costs £3,300 per page. By directing the advertising runs the designer can control the way his product is presented to the public, and does not have to rely on the interpretations of a fashion editor. Once the goods are placed in the stores, it's also my job to check quality, presentation, window displays and display material.

'It's necessary to have a staggered programme. It wouldn't be a good idea to flood the market with several Bruce Oldfield products simultaneously. A spectacle frame will undergo many more trials and retrials for strength and comfort than a swimsuit, and therefore the "tooling up" process takes longer. The design input for a range of sheets is obviously less than for sportswear. So the lead-in time for sample products has to be worked out and carefully timed. 'During the development of the product, Bruce has to work with the companies' in-house technicians and designers. He will make visits to Nottingham or Belfast for Charnos, Oregon or Newcastle for Nike, and Copenhagen for Birger Christensen furs. He has to make himself available for promotional activities, such as talking to sales forces at sales conferences and attending product launches with both press and buyers.

In September 1986, for instance, he made a trip to Washington for the launch of the American Simplicity Style pattern range.

'These are very important benefits for the licensee. They have the use of a top designer's name. Their range of products is extended, too – not to mention their profits. Licensing is a practice that benefits everyone involved.'

It's a business extension that has pleased Bruce enormously. 'My first collection for Charnos hosiery was really aimed at "un"designing the tights after the previous season's craze for fussy texturing, and the sales were excellent. I'm perfectly happy for a customer to buy my hosiery for Charnos or my shoes for Rayne and put them with a Saint Laurent dress. I don't expect my customers to be head-to-toe from one designer. It looks as if they haven't done much thinking! On the other hand, there are also many of our customers who are very busy women. They don't have time to pick and co-ordinate their clothes from several different sources. So, in the shop, we can provide them with almost everything they need, clothes and accessories. I want them to have the broadest possible options under the Bruce Oldfield name, and to recognise that there is a look there that can be applied to anything they wear. I also find it very rewarding to design a shoe, a dress, a tennis dress all in one day. Design themes from one area can be moved into another, be adapted, and spark off yet another idea.

'In this country fashion licensing has only recently begun, yet every major American, French and Italian designer uses it to subsidise those vast expensive fashion shows and their big runs of advertising. The licensees look at it like this: if they present themselves

in the most glamorous way with a top designer, top
models, top venues, the best accessories and the best
glossy advertising, everyone gains. The press can
hardly fail to devote column inches to the show, the
customer is impressed, the image gets stronger, the
company grows. Few in the audience of a big
international fashion show stop to count up, but you
will probably find that the sweaters, furs, shoes,
sunglasses, hosiery, shirts and leathers by the
designer are made by other companies through licence
deals. That designer might only have made up one third
of the garments in the show. It all goes to attract the
customer at the end of the line.

'Today, licensing revenue funds my big runs of
advertising. And it will allow me to open another shop
next year without borrowing thousands of pounds
from the bank. I would like to have a Bruce Oldfield
store where you could buy everything I design, with
the clothes as the central factor. I'm very careful that
whatever I take on is a logical expansion of the main
core of my business, which is fashion. I have been
building up to this point for many years, collecting a
good team, structuring a solid business that is here to
stay, and I think I can say the moment has arrived to
capitalise on that.'

Bruce Oldfield *for Rayne*

In early December 1985, Nicholas and Edward Rayne, assistant managing directors of the H & M Rayne Shoe Manufacturing Company, approached Bruce Oldfield to suggest that they should work together on a shoe collection. A family firm one century old, Rayne started as a theatrical costumier and once made shoes for Lily Langtry, Edward VII's mistress, and dressed Diaghilev's Russian Ballet. The Rayne factory makes shoes for all the Rayne shops and for world export. Nicholas Rayne sees Bruce Oldfield as occupying the same slot in fashion as Rayne do in shoes – expensive, up-market and specialising in dressy day and evening wear.

'Naturally, we keep a close watch on the Paris and London shows to see which way fashion is moving, and we are very aware of the high-profile designers. Thirty or forty years ago we started to make Christian Dior shoe collections, and since then we have been on the look-out for exceptionally talented designers with names that are internationally known. We sell heavily to the USA, where name-recognition means a lot. The design input is very important, for obviously shoes will only sell when they are keyed in to the new directions in fashion. Bruce Oldfield was a happy choice because he satisfies our criteria, because our customer profiles are complementary, and because he is British, which enables us to offer a wholly British product.'

There were four initial business meetings to organise parameters and working methods before the contract was signed. Bruce picked the basic shoe shapes from Rayne's library of shoe 'lasts', wooden prototypes around which a shoe design is built. He then sketched a large number of ideas and transferred his chosen designs on to the plastic cut-outs supplied by Rayne: plastic shells shaped from the lasts and formed into three-dimensional shoe shapes on a vacuum-forming machine. He draws on these with a spirit-based pen, and can pin or staple on pieces of fabric or trimming. The first seven design shells are taken to the factory on Wednesday 8 January. Bruce discusses them with Lulu Rayne, stock merchandise controller and wife of Nicholas, chief designer Jean Matthews, designer Melbo Kkafas, and any of the machine operators they may call in for a technical assessment. From here, the next stage is for Rayne to make up the chosen designs. Once the shoe has gone into production, Rayne order fabric or leather from Bruce's suppliers. Their pattern cutter will form a paper pattern from the plastic shell, and send it through to the cutters. The cutters make a fabric pattern, or a leather pattern; each requires a different

THE SHELLS

BREASTING – TRIMMING THE SOLE

HAND-CLEANING THE FINISHED SHOE

A FINAL POLISH

technique. This pattern then leaves the clicking room (i.e. the cutting room) and goes to the closing room to be stitched together into an upper. When stitched, it is flat: the shoe is then lasted, or shaped, in the lasting room and finished in the shoe room.

'We continually modify, change, and drop,' explains Lulu Rayne. 'Shoes not only have to look good, they have to be comfortable.' Among the fifty-five employees at the factory they have every shoe size from 3 to 12 (American), and they test-wear the shoes themselves. Mrs Rayne is their 7B tester: Edie, the telephonist, is the 8½ tester.

The sample, size 7B American or 5½ English, is taken to the shoe shows in Milan in early March, just before the fashion shows. If the buyers place an order, it will be graded up, or sized accordingly. For instance, Japan sells E widths, unknown in Britain, and Texans buy 4A widths for exceptionally narrow feet. 'It's a status thing,' says Nicholas Rayne. 'Texans believe narrow feet to be aristocratic.'

The first problem that holds up the meeting on 8 January is a shoe of pleated lamé. Bruce Oldfield has brought along a sample he has used for a lamé dress. Mrs Rayne points out the pleats won't hold, the fabric will smooth out in the making. Bruce suggests it could be flat-backed – in other words, pleated on to a backer first. The trouble then is that it would be three layers thick, which could make the shoe look bulky. Jean Matthews, who has been with the company for thirty years, is asked to look at it. She shakes her head. 'That lamé weave is too open. The glue we use in manufacturing would come through.'

Bruce decides to take it one stage further. He will go back to his fabric supplier and ask them to pleat it on to a suitable backer. He will send it over to Rayne to try out. They look at some more designs: a wrapover with bows tied on the side, a few with details such as rococo plaster curls on the side and the heel, and one which has a front lace insertion like a décollétage.

The lace insertion is difficult. Jean Matthews points out that it would rip and tear in the machine. She suggests mounting the lace on clear plastic, and then abandons the idea because it would tear along the stitching line. Perhaps they should do it by hand. The idea worries Lulu Rayne, because it means holding up production. 'Let's have some lace, and we'll experiment,' she tells Bruce.

She has asked him to look at some plastic they have which is printed with a lace effect. He finds that although it is better than he expected it to be, it is still too heavy-looking and the background colour too evident. He intends to see his designs carried through as closely as possible to his original conceptions and is continuously, although courteously, on his guard against easy substitutes.

The rococo trimmings for the back of the heel and the sides are straightforward. It is decided that Bruce will get them made up in India by the embroiderer he uses for his dresses, send them over, and Rayne will attach them as appliqués. The only problem is that they must be made to curve with the angle of the foot, so Lulu Rayne arranges for him to receive two finished shoes to work on, one with a high and one with a low heel.

Finally they discuss the leather tie which looks like a scarf knot at the side of the shoe. An actual knot would be too bulky, so it will have to be faked. Bruce writes down six things he must do before the next meeting, and promises several more designs.

DISCUSSIONS WITH
LULU RAYNE

Of the seven original designs, five went through to the sample stage. The lamé pleats, sent over from Bruce's supplier on a backer, were too bulky. However, by stripping off the backing and applying another backing of their own, Rayne found a way to make the shoe work and it was included in the collection. The lace insertion shoe was tried out in a number of different ways, but proved to be too fragile: it was dropped, along with one other design which worked technically but looked too clumsy.

Nicholas Rayne looks at the Bruce Oldfield line as a long-term project, 'because of the long lead-in time, six months from the plastic shells to the finished shoes selling in the shops. Each collection overlaps with the next and we expect it to take at least two years to become fully lucrative. The first collection was designed in a rush in January so the shoes could not be ready for New York in February, but we were able to show them in Milan, Düsseldorf and London. The next collection went through smoothly and sold about as well as we had anticipated – not bad, considering it is a slow time in the US economy and exchange rate fluctuations have depressed the market still further. By the third collection we'll be selling shoes in four continents and it should begin to take off.

'In any case, Bruce Oldfield's name adds a sparkle and glamour to our range and helps bridge the gap between shoe and clothes sales – something that pleases everyone.'

THE FINISHED RANGE

Bruce Oldfield *for Birger Christensen*

Jens Birger Christensen, director of Birger
Christensen the fur company:
'We have had our shop at 170 New Bond Street for three
years, and have been great admirers of Bruce Oldfield's
image and styling. The London Label Fur Group put me
in touch with him because, although we already carry
certain very well-known international designer
collections such as Kenzo, Claude Montana and Ralph
Lauren, we had no English designer to put forward.
'I wrote Bruce a letter, and he was immediately
positive. We signed the contract on our second
meeting. He will design an annual collection for us of
fifteen toiles, three of them leather. Bruce immediately
went to Copenhagen to choose skins and discuss ideas
with our designer Christina Frycklund. She is our
fashion adviser and has all the technical knowledge at
her fingertips; she can explain why you do not put a long-
haired fur with a flat-haired one, or show how a toile
has to be cut larger for a fur coat than a silk one. Bruce
Oldfield already knew something about furs and picked
it up very quickly. He was particularly interested in the
highly skilful work involved in making a fur coat. A
mink pelt, for example, is fifteen inches long: it is cut
into small diagonal strips, which are then meticulously
reassembled to preserve the continuity of the mink
stripe and other features of the fur. The end result is a
fabric of fur rather than an assembly of pelts. The
construction of a fur coat is completely different from
that of a cloth coat. You have to be extraordinarily
careful about weight, bulk and line.
'Bruce then came back and made some drawings and
came to see us with the toiles. We tried them on a model
and discussed them with our fitter and pattern cutter

Arthur Hinsley. We made some alterations which Bruce
approved on the second fitting – a bigger cuff, more of
a sweep. The third fitting was in fur, after which only
things like length and closings can be changed. For the
subsequent collections Bruce will go to Copenhagen.
'As the first collection takes five months to prepare, it's
a little early to assess sales. But we have sold fifteen
pieces and our customers say his coats are "dressy and
different". We gradually build up the designer
collections, adding to them year by year. They don't
go out of date as quickly as other clothes.
'Bruce Oldfield's styling with our manufacturing,
distribution and sales outlets in the USA, Japan and
Europe – how can we lose?'

'THE CONSTRUCTION OF
A FUR COAT IS COMPLETE-
LY DIFFERENT ... YOU
HAVE TO BE EXTRAORDIN-
ARILY CAREFUL ABOUT
WEIGHT, BULK AND LINE'

FITTING THE TOILE:
'TOO HEAVY IN MINK –
TRY IT IN BROADTAIL?'

PLACING THE LEAF
MOTIF

Bruce Oldfield *for Charnos*

John Roskalns, marketing manager of Charnos Hosiery:

'This is the first time Charnos have linked their name with that of a designer. Like Charnos, the Bruce Oldfield name stands for a flattering, feminine, classical look. At a time when we are expanding into the continental market it is a great advantage that his name is well known in the better boutiques and stores where we want to make our impact.

'Every packet of stockings or tights says "Bruce Oldfield for Charnos", but when we looked at his designs we had already decided to forget all about the name and just consider them on their own merits. And the buyers tell us that these lines would have sold well anyway, because they are refreshingly clean and simple after all the jazzy cut-and-sew lace jobs of last winter. We backed the new collection with a brochure photographed by top beauty photographer John Swannell showing the tights as part of a whole Oldfield look. So far we've sold fifty per cent more than we targeted for, so we are more than pleased with the results.

'The bonus is that Bruce is superb to work with, businesslike and quick and easy to reach. We had to accelerate to bring the collection out in October for the Christmas season, and with a less efficient designer I don't think we could have done it.

'We've recently taken him to our lingerie factory with a view to a further Oldfield collection in that range. He has gone away to see where there is a gap in the marketplace. Beauty and glamour are not the whole story. We also want to sell items within an accessible price range. Bruce's down-to-earth approach will, I think, make this a real possibility for next year.'

BRUCE, ANITA AND JOHN ROSKALNS IN THE CHARNOS FACTORY

PERSONAL APPEARANCE AT HARRODS

Bruce Oldfield *for Nike*

John Trainor, head of European marketing in Nike, the worldwide US-based sportswear company:

'The Bruce Oldfield collection is a big departure for Nike. The company began fifteen years ago as a very serious, functional, masculine-sports oriented brand. Philip Knight, the chairman, was a college athlete and he sold properly structured running shoes out of the back of a car at races with his coach Bill Bowman: and then it grew! We have never known how to approach women's sportswear. At the same time we made up our minds that we didn't want to go for the purely functional, hardline image that you get, say, with Martina Navratilova and Puma.

'The choice we had, once we had decided to make sportswear for women, was to employ someone and start from the beginning or go straight to a top international designer who already had a reputation for a feminine, sophisticated look. It only took one meeting with Bruce Oldfield to convince everyone he was a great designer and a strong and likeable personality. I think we feared a superstar temperament – and of course he is shrewd, businesslike and his head is screwed on very firmly, although he likes to kid you that the financial details don't interest him. So we signed a three-year contract.

'The first collection is for on and off the tennis court, with a few pairs of shoes. Bruce made up the toiles and five of us went along to see them in Wimbledon week, when our American staff were over here. We took one look and thought if they look that good in calico, they're going to look bloody marvellous when they are finished. He had a very strong view of what the outfits ought to do. He talked about Carole Lombard and the 1930s, he wanted the clothes to have a bit of cleavage and be sexy, he cut the knickers in with the dress so the shape would be streamlined, and he thought of details such as necklines which would frame the Beverly Hills necklaces.

'He then got together with Mary Bodecker, the US/UK Nike link, over fabrics, and made up the samples which were approved over here. We are sourcing, or manufacturing, here in the UK for distribution at selected outlets round the world. There'll be an import duty for the US to pay, but with such a prestigious and expensive line that's the last concern. They'll be launched in spring 1988, and we'll be approaching the buyers in early October.'

9

'How

many times

must

I tell you?

The

chic woman

doesn't

plunge.'

EDITING
THE WINTER COLLECTION

It is Monday 10 February, 1.30 p.m. With thirty-three days to the show and seventy-seven colour crayon sketches up on the board, it is time to edit the collection.

Bruce Oldfield's priority is the balance, crucial in any Oldfield collection, between late day and evening. It is important to show seventy per cent dressy day and cocktail wear to thirty per cent evening wear, or the buyers may go away with the impression that Oldfield is too grand and beyond the lifestyle of their customers. He must also maintain the continuity between spring and winter so that there isn't a 'season jump' and the vagaries of the weather can be overcome by offering a variety of suitable weights. A further consideration is to make sure the new lines are developed and worked into the Oldfield 'look'. Generally, couture ideas and themes are developed for the ready-to-wear of the following season.

Anita Richardson's role is to make sure the best sellers of the previous season are being replaced by probable best sellers for winter. She is also there to chivvy Bruce over dates and to edit down, knowing that he will be injecting new dresses up to the last minute. With prices between around £280 and £3,000 retail, cutting costs is not a priority, but Anita must ensure that there is a balance in the range of prices offered. She will keep an eye on just how many outfits have expensive additions such as fur and embroidery. One of her main concerns is to see that Bruce offers jersey dresses in depth. Oldfield customers will buy three or four of them a season, and at about £300 they are a bargain within the Oldfield price bracket. The buyers would be disappointed not to find a big jersey group in the show, but Bruce tends to include the minimum and pass on to something more challenging.

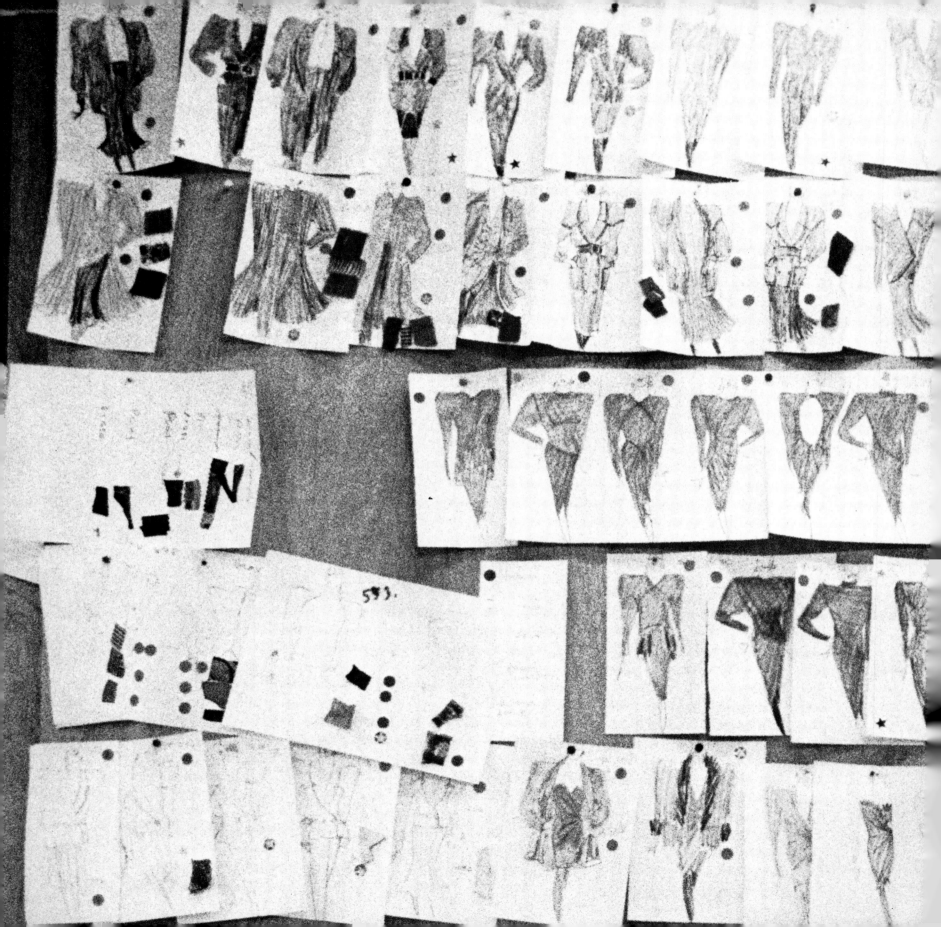

At present the workrooms are crammed with garments and fabrics. There are ten rails of dresses in the stockroom, representing the previous three and a half months' manufacturing. Some will go straight into the shop for spring the following Monday, 17 February, the day marking the end of the protracted winter 1985 sale. The rest are orders for export and for Harvey Nichols. Four fifths of the £250,000-worth of fabrics are stock for the made-to-measure customers, and export orders already taken; and the balance are the new fabrics, mostly ordered at Frankfurt, for sampling. The majority of the new fabrics will appear on the catwalk and be reordered by the company according to buyers' demands.

Bruce and Anita have cleared the afternoon's appointments, have asked the receptionist not to put calls through, and now settle down in front of the board. Bruce lights a cigarette and sits sideways at the worktop where he sketched the designs they are now scrutinising. 'We'll aim at eighty garments for the show,' he says. Anita asks how many are already under way. 'We–ell,' says Bruce, 'all the leathers, a few in spring fabrics for the shop and of course the beading and embroidery. Say, one fifth.'

They look at the board for a few minutes in complete silence, one of them puffing at the cigarette, the other munching a sandwich. Bruce pulls himself out of his trance with a jerk.

'Look at the first eight. All leather, three jackets, two with lamb collars. You've got every element: short tight skirt, gored skirt, one trouser. There's nothing to stop the buyer putting A together with B, and so on.'

'I think people can be pretty lazy about putting together different combinations,' says Anita.

'Then we can't be,' says Bruce. 'We'll show them how.'
They move on to a group of coat-dresses in wool crêpe.
'These styles are all finished, the lamé, the dot and the
check fabrics. These are the fabrics I want, but they're
not in yet.'
'I'll chase it,' says Anita. 'Is that lined? I think it needs
it for winter.'
Bruce gets up, walks around and stabs the board five or
six times with his finger. 'That draping is very
important,' he says. He is thinking himself into
presentation, and has begun to talk like the press release
that will be supplied to the audience at his show. 'It
comes through many, many times, sometimes in lamé, as
in a tunic or long dress.'
'And that one, number six on the second row. What's
that?'
'Leather and silk. It's one of the Birger Christensen
numbers. They're making them in Copenhagen.'
Anita makes a frightened face. 'Where will we keep the
furs before the show?'
'Don't even think about them,' says Bruce. '£200,000-
worth. They won't get to London until the day
before. Christ knows where we'll keep them. They'd
better stay in New Bond Street. Christensen are insured,
we're not.'
He takes a step back and squints at the colours.
'I'm planning the show to begin in brown and black and
go into bronze and cream.'
Anita waves the stub end of her sandwich at him. 'Just
to go off at a tangent, shall we get some Charnos tights
specially done? And what about the shoes?'
'I'm doing that collection for Rayne,' he says. 'So we'll
use their shoes in the show.'
The shoes for the show are an immediate headache.

LONG DRESS,
WOOL CRÊPE
WITH BULLION

BLACK VELVET:
STRAPLESS DRESS
UNDER FLARED
COAT

BLACK WOOL JERSEY,
ASYMMETRIC RED
DRAPES

Although the twenty or so model girls Bruce will be using are all size 10, their feet could vary from 4½ to 7½. The shoes will be credited to the shoemaker in the programme, and for that reason they are sometimes given free and sometimes charged wholesale at around £40 a pair. The models will need day and evening shoes, which could bring the bill to around £1,600. And as the shoes have to be made specially, in fabrics to go with the collection and in specified sizes, the models have to be booked first. At present, only ten are confirmed.

Bruce begins to collect rolls of fabric from the corners of the room and stack them below the drawings. 'These are the wool crêpes and gold bullion,' he explains, pointing to a section of designs in row three.

Anita wipes her fingers on a handkerchief. 'There are a lot of dresses, Bruce. I think we should add in a few separates down there. In fact, why not make that whole group separates?'

Bruce is taken aback. He studies the group of drawings narrowly. 'You can be top-to-toe for much less in a dress,' he points out. Then he changes the subject abruptly. 'All these styles here are jersey. I know you like jersey. Clever use of colour. And you can have your warm winter numbers.'

Anita laughs. 'May I remind you that Harvey Nichols bought eighty per cent jersey last time. It's bread and butter for the serious buyers. We got through five or six pieces of coral last time, even though the Americans just bought flash. And, by the way, there's nothing plunging.'

'You old tart. 253 was our best seller last time and it was right up to the chin.'

Anita instantly comes back: '279 was a plunger! That did well!'

'Yeah, but that was an evening dress. How many times must I tell you? The chic woman doesn't plunge. And it is the *winter*, you know.' But Bruce is nearly defeated. Anita takes a more general stand. 'We will order three dozen for the shop and probably repeat two dozen later.'

Bruce is still worried. 'But these designs don't go with bare necks. You know what happens. These shoulder pads start toppling about and the neck starts falling all over the place, it's a bloody nightmare.'

He sits on the stool and makes a smacking sound with his lips.

'You want plunging jerseys, do you?'

'369 was a plunge! A wrap job!'

'Well, look at the bottom line. Plenty of evening plunge.'

Anita asks, 'So which is the replacement to 253, then?'

'I don't know. Maybe the brown and purple, the two reds and the blue. Basic sexy shapes. Four right little winners.'

He moves on to the last row of sketches. 'Fitted jacket, big jacket, coat-dress for evening. Topstitched in beading.'

Anita: 'How do they manage the lapels? You can't top stitch those, surely?'

'Yes you can. He beads along the edge, and they simply machine the lapel seam, using a zipper foot.'

'I wondered about the weight of the beads.'

'It'll be OK; there will only be two rows of bugle beads.' They talk in shorthand, then lapse into silence again. Bruce sits back, tapping his teeth with a pencil. When George brings in the tea, she finds the room in total silence.

Almost as an aside, Bruce says, 'You think those jerseys should be matt?'

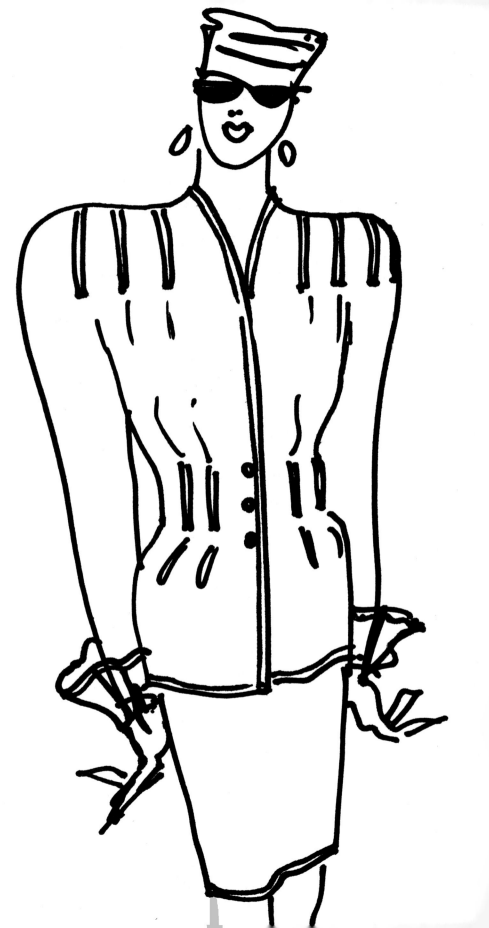

SUITS: PLAIN LEATHER,
LEOPARD SPOT LAMÉ BLOUSE;
STAMPED LEATHER, WAISTED
JACKET

JERSEY DRESS: TAFFETA
JACKET AND COAT WITH
WOOL JERSEY PANTS

Ruched velvet

full Taff Skirts

bulk out with net.

Mink Collar -
Burger
Christenson

wrap front -
covered buttons

Very full Skirts -
perhaps a slight
train

Rayne Velvet
Shoe -

EVENING DRESSES:
RUCHED AND CRUSHED
VELVETS WITH TAFFETA
AND MINK, PRINT
SEQUINS

off-shoulder
mink collar -
use males.

overskirt let
into hip seam -

Very full
overskirt + train

wrap underskirt
very slim —

mink trimmed
shoe.

cap sleeve
cut to flute.

All draped
from central
panel.

Scallop for
print sequins.

C.F. Fluted

'Definitely.'

'OK, OK, I know you are always telling me there's more opportunity to wear those than anything else.'

The tea re-energises Bruce. 'The first six', he says, getting up to indicate the final group of grand evening dresses, 'are shot taffetas.'

'They're goodies. For the style, the show and the selling. I can see them on the catwalk.'

Bruce is piqued. 'I can see it *all* on the catwalk.'

'I know,' says Anita. 'You're the designer. Is that taffeta coat lined?'

'I thought I'd line it with wool jersey. Nice with taffeta.'

'I can't picture it.'

'I can. Just a coat lined in wool. Then a wool jersey top and a chiffon skirt. We've got to have a few different things.'

'Are we going to cost them backwards now?'

'Certainly not,' says Bruce. 'The wool jerseys are OK.'

Anita calculates. '£400 a dress?'

'With beading, £550. The basic cloth is a good price and it's wide. Even the silk crêpes will come in at around £600 retail.'

'How much are the embroidery additions?'

Bruce names a sum.

'That's what I call a lot.'

Bruce grins. 'That's one sleeve. You want two?'

'Just remember,' says Anita, 'You're adding on £300 for embroidery before you start the dress.'

'I think I'll do some more separates. We'll need some more variety in this section.'

'Fifteen long dresses?'

'I thought twenty. I did think of doing a bright finale, a nice big red section. I've already got all those muted silks.'

'And there's the gauze. What are you going to do with that?'

'Keep it for private customers,' says Bruce. The gauze will join the fabrics kept as alternative stock for the made-to-measure department, on offer to the private customers.

Bruce pulls two pieces of bugle bead embroidery out of a box under his desk. 'One was done by hand. The other was done by a machine at a third of the price. Which is which?'

Anita can't tell. She turns back to the board, considering one of the most flamboyant parts of the show. 'The section that we haven't got yet is the gala extroverts.'

'That's what I'm working on. Those fabrics are the fabrics I've been pulling out.'

They try to take out some of the numbers. Anita argues, Bruce shakes his head.

'I was wondering,' says Anita with caution. 'Have we gone too heavily into velvet?'

Bruce considers. 'Number 5 we won't have anyway, because I've only got two mink linings. 1 and 4 are both for long as well, so maybe I'll just do them in long. You'd get more wear out of the cocktail, but it's better value for money if it's long. I dunno. This one is a real showpiece; but technically it might not work out.'

There are many reasons why a design might be dropped at any stage between drawing board and finished sample. It might prove too difficult to perfect and finish in the time available, or the fabric might not arrive by the promised date. The finished sample might not fit in with one of the groups that add up to the look of the collection, or the 'story' doesn't come over strongly enough.

BULLION JACKET WITH
PEPLUM AND LOW FRONT:
PANTS

SHIRRED PANNÉ VELVET
DRESS, CHIFFON SKIRT

BROADTAIL SUIT
WITH SATIN LAPELS

WOOL CRÊPE AND
BULLION DRESS,
WATERFALL FRONT

Anita is still concerned that Bruce hasn't put in enough evenings. 'You've got a lot of day things, except they've got bead additions.'

Bruce deliberates. 'I would say there are fifteen things which are cocktail, twenty long dresses, fifteen separates. I think it's enough. Because of all that leather. Bruce Oldfield makes leather. It's an expensive day thing which you can also wear in the evening. For the stores we'll be offering more than flash. They can sell twice as many late days as evenings. They're being offered a wide selection of clothing.'

'Yes, but last time we went too heavily into day wear. And we don't want to frighten them off.'

'We've got to give a choice to the wholesale buyer,' says Bruce. 'That shop in Boston, for instance, that doesn't buy evening wear. But I agree we can't stock it all ourselves. There aren't that many styles. It's more variations in trim and repeats over different fabrics.'

'Incidentally,' says Anita, with sudden emphasis, 'let's go through the fabrics that haven't come in yet.'

'That's right. It's 10 February, for God's sake, and the show is 15 March. I mean to say, it's a bit *slack*.'

If the samples aren't in in time for the show, those fabrics won't become part of the collection: 'We'll telex ''Cancel all outstanding orders'',' says Anita. They go through the Frankfurt sample book, and Anita phones for the stocking-in book, meticulously kept by Angus, the stockroom manager. They find that from one fabric firm alone, five out of eleven fabrics are not logged in as arrived.

'The plain is in, here, but the print that goes with it hasn't arrived.'

Anita shrugs. 'Cancel the whole family and send back the plains.'

Having made notes, Anita looks at her watch. 'All
right, shall I get out of your way now?'
Bruce takes a last look at the board. 'We're going to end
up with 100 outfits, you know. Some will hit the dust,
but I've got quite a lot to add.'
'And I know you. With three days to go you'll be
starting a new group.'
It is three hours since they began to assess the
collection, and there are still seventy-seven designs on
the board. On the positive side, they have extended the
probable best sellers, Bruce has picked out most of
the fabrics he will use for his evening finale, and they
have saved some money by cancelling the late fabrics.
They are one step nearer to the final collection.

10

PLANNING
THE
SHOW

CASTING

Height 5′9½ Dress Size 10–12 Bust 33 Waist 23 Hips 34 Shoes 6½ Hair Dark Auburn Eyes Dark Brown
Grösse 1.76 Konfektion 38 Oberweite 84 Taille 58 Hüfte 86 Schuhe 39 Haare Dunkelkastanie Augen Dunkelbraun
SHOWS

Amanda
Janelle
Deena
Kal
Jane Spencer
Anna Curtis

Tania
Jane Catherine
Yvonne
Cathy Brooks
Marva
Robin
Linda
Arianne
Marie
Pat
Hazel
Lynne.

At 1 p.m. on Wednesday, 19 February, two models are waiting in Bruce Oldfield's Fulham premises to see Bruce. One has a sheep's nose and full lips, the other has large amber eyes and blue-black hair: both are around six feet tall. Bruce is talking on the phone to a customer who is leaving for Australia with a dozen Oldfield frocks in her luggage.

'I was there a month ago for the Bond wedding,' he is saying. 'I was doing the dress for Alan Bond's daughter – he's the chap who funded the Australian team when they won the America's Cup. It was a seriously grand wedding. I mean, there were 2,500 people being held back by the police . . . No, you've got just the right things. Perth is a laid-back outdoorsy life. The kitchen opens out into the pool, you know, and there's an indoor discothèque next to the jacuzzi area. The houses there all look like luxury offices, with smoked glass, magnificent views. No, it's fab. You'll have a great time.'

He swivels on his architect's stool. 'Hi, girls! Let's have your pictures, then.' He flips through the models' portfolios while George sorts out their agency cards printed with the measurements and showing a close up, a 'natural' outside shot and a sophisticated number in evening dress.

'OK,' says Bruce, 'out with the measuring tape!' George encircles the first model's skinny chest and calls out, 'Thirty-two!'

The model makes a face. 'Overawed, aren't you?'

'Shoe size? American's one and a half sizes up, isn't it? Right! Thanks! Next! You're Donna, aren't you? I've seen you do shows.'

Donna looks pleased. 'He's not just a cute face, is he?' she says to George.

GEORGE, TAPE MEASURE
AT THE READY

BRUCE SCRUTINISES A
MODEL'S PORTFOLIO

Two men enter the room, one small and bald with bright black eyes swimming behind strong-lensed glasses, the other tall and chiselled in a baggy jacket. They are Mikel Rosen and Russell Marsh of Mikel Rosen Productions, a firm which stages special fashion shows around the world. They also run their own PR company. Mikel Rosen and Bruce Oldfield have been friends since art school days and Mikel's company organised the Barnardo's gala show with great success two years ago. They drop plastic bags of video tapes on the floor.

'Hullo, everyone. We've asked twenty girls to turn up today, but we'll be lucky if we see fifteen. We've just done a count of who's booked, and we're half way there. And there will be girls coming in at the last minute because you're not sure whether some of the star people will come or not. But if you want Pat Cleveland, no one else will do!'

'She's a real actress and she can play any role,' says Bruce. 'You don't have to tell her what to do . . . and she's polite!'

'She's just a moon-faced child but she's the greatest model alive,' says Mikel, dreamily.

Donna's voice breaks in, flat and bored. 'Do you need us any more?' she asks coldly.

'No thanks! We'll be in touch.'

While Russell lays out jewellery on Bruce's worktop, Mikel recaps on arrangements for the show.

'We're much better off with the hall you've got because we'll have time to set up the back of the stage so that it's an individual statement. You don't get an opportunity in the tents, not when you're sharing with nine other designers. I think we should make the show very fast and crisp. It's just boring for the press to sit through a long show – after all, there's over 100

MIKEL, RUSSELL AND BRUCE: 'WE'VE ASKED TWENTY GIRLS TO TURN UP TODAY, BUT WE'LL BE LUCKY IF WE SEE FIFTEEN'

A CLUTCH OF BARBARIC METAL PENDANTS AND CHAINS. RUSSELL AND BRUCE EXAMINING THE JEWELLERY

designers trying to be unforgettable in four days.
How do you take that seriously?'

'I'm finished,' says Russell. 'This is by Jennifer Corker
of Corker and Currie.' He indicates a clutch of
barbaric metal pendants and chains.

'They've done things for Bodymap before,' explains
Mikel, 'but they've left that behind now. These are Lisa
Vandy. You know those clips for an ear or a nostril? She
did those. She could do something special for you. To be
basic, though, Corker and Currie are cheaper. We
could borrow from their stock.'

'I should hope *so*.' Bruce lifts up one of Corker and
Currie's beaten silver earrings with rampant lions. 'Is
it titanium? You know, we could use these metal letters
to spell out GLAM and GLITZY and CHIC, and chain
them together. That would be a real good showpiece. I
could see us selling this in the shop. The stuff for the
show wouldn't be just an empty gesture, we could sell
it all season.' He parts two slats of the Venetian blind
and peers down into the yard. 'Here's another girl at
the door. This one's a bit heavy, I think.'

'It's Nikki,' says Mikel. 'She was in Fashion Aid. You
saw her in the YSL finale, wearing the mauve dress.'

'The big taffeta job? Hullo there! In here.'
Bruce casts a sceptical eye over the measurements on
the model's card, and then remeasures. '33-25-36.'

'Thirty-*three*?' screams the model. 'Thirty-*six*?'

'The agency has been massaging the statistics again!
Naughty, naughty! Here it says 34-24-35.' The model
leaves, protesting, and they turn back to Lisa Vandy's
heavy crafted metalwork, necklaces with egg-size beads
and earrings chained together round the nape of the
neck.

'These are nice, but a bit laid-back for the show.'

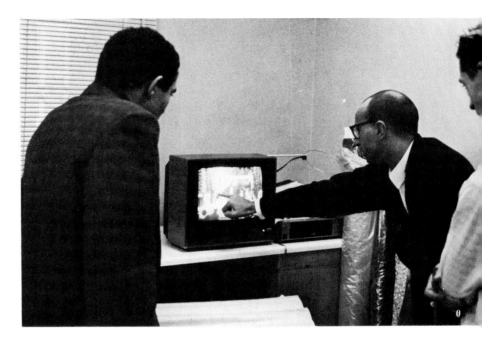

'WATCH WHAT THE
MODELS ARE DOING,
IT'S A NICE ATTITUDE'

Five girls arrive together, all with an Oriental or half-caste look: slanting eyes, full lips and Louise Brooks hair. Tania from Los Angeles breasts into the tape measure.

'Everyone takes these really tight measurements and then when it's time to get into a tight frock . . . oh boy!'

Bruce surveys the girls. 'Well, you all look very good together with your bobs. You – sorry, Anna – have you done any shows? Two? Because at the moment I think we'd have a problem with your height. Mostly I have girls who are five feet nine upwards. You're a good two inches shorter than the others. Thanks for coming in, anyway. And Carrie, how old are you? Sixteen? Because you look even younger to me. My clothes are quite grown up and I think you would need to be a little older. See you next year, yes?'

Mikel slots in a video. 'I want you to see this new girl called Janelle. Fast forward . . . there.' They trawl through model books sent by agencies on behalf of girls who are abroad or working today. In between, Mikel fills Bruce in on plans to mirror a back wall for the show, to be brought in and fixed at the end of the catwalk at 7 a.m. on the fifteenth.

Pat brings in the tea at 4 p.m. and Mikel sums up.

'We've got Annette, Amanda, Dina, Jane. There's Janelle and Jan.'

'Pass on Jan,' says Bruce.

'OK. There's Arianne, she's the one who was in *Year of the Dragon* and there's Tarita. Michele makes eight. Divina and Ivonska, ten. Then there are the celebs, Pat, Marie Helvin, Hazel Collins, thirteen. What are we looking for? Sixteen?'

'This is what we have to talk about. We need to see which girls we bunch together and which go out on their own. And I want you to go through the shoe sizes one more time with George.' Bruce looks at the diary. 'We have to give Rayne all the sizes by Monday. We've done the mirror, done the jewellery, what else is there?'

Just as they are packing up, two more models arrive. Bruce knows the first girl, a Swede so pale she's almost transparent. He takes the briefest look at her book, confirms her measurements and says, 'Fantastico! You're on!'

The second girl gets a rather different reception.

'Is this a fitting or a casting?' she asks.

'Why?' says Bruce. 'Are you working out how much you can charge me?'

'No, it's just that I won't be here later. I'm going to Paris and Milan, and I won't be back until Fashion Week.'

'That's quite all right,' says Bruce, silkily. 'If I've got you right, you are the pain in the ass who stayed in Paris last time and failed to turn up or let us know.'

'No, I didn't,' says the model vengefully. 'I was phoning up for days and couldn't get to speak to anybody. Everybody was busy, so I gave up.'

Bruce is whistling to himself and doing a sketch.

'So you don't need me for a fitting?'

'You're not needed at all, actually.'

PLANNING
THE
SHOW

PRODUCTION

It is early evening on Wednesday 26 February when Mikel and Russell arrive at Bruce's flat. The planning of the show is under way. They are to spend a few hours choosing the music which will go towards creating the mood of the show, and which will accompany particular groups of clothes: they will watch videos, looking for ideas on choreography and special effects; and they need to decide and order the spotlight colour gels which light the catwalk. George, Bruce's assistant, is also present. As the door opens for Mikel and Russell, Bruce is vacuuming the oatmeal carpet. 'Hang on!' he says. 'I'm being a housewife!'

Mikel and Russell tip albums, tapes and videos on to the floor with a welter of running sheets, the forms which list the order of the models on the catwalk. 'I've been speaking to the agencies all day, sorting out the fees,' says Russell to Bruce, who is putting away the vacuum and getting out a bottle of champagne. Mikel accepts a glass, and begins sorting and loading videos. 'Here we go. Watch what the models are doing, because it's a nice attitude. This is the Richmond Cornejo show we did in Tokyo. The music's Hitchcock – *Psycho*. You see . . . they keep just drifting around as if they didn't know where they were going. Then more girls come crowding in behind like ghosts. Now the lighting comes in. Here's the designer. He came on like that because he wanted to be there to make sure the models did what he wanted them to do.'

'Prima donna!' says Bruce to George, ready with her notebook. 'But that's OK. I quite like the drifting around.'

'Watch this,' says Mikel, 'when they start walking forward. Now the blue starts spilling out of there . . . just a floating around feeling, with sexy clothes. Now the light fades away and you hear drumming. This is where the lights go on, off, on, off.'

'You can't see the *clothes*!'

'Look,' Mikel fiddles with the contrast button. 'Now they are coming out face-to-face in pairs, like you had them in Fashion Aid.'

'I'm not crazy about that face-to-face thing. Done that! Been there!'

Mikel is intent on the fast forward button. 'This is Bernstock Spiers.'

'How are they doing?'

'Really well, after that bad season. It's gone really sophisticated this time. It's called ''All Woman''. That's why we did it very grown up and static in Tokyo. Now watch! They took the models off and put them in singlets and boxer shorts like American sports clothes. They looked like yobbos. Now! This is the best ever! Michael Clark showed them how to dance. The Japanese went crazy for it! Pat Cleveland could do what that girl's doing. She drags off the model in fur and sequins – just drags her off the catwalk! The two of them tussle on stage! I just want you to see the laser and mirrors now.'

'Give me a BREAK!' cries Bruce. 'And this music! Let's face it, those buyers will have been hearing that alternative crap all week. Wait a minute, back a bit, who is that girl?'

The video tape stops on the impassive, sleepy face of a peachy black girl floating along a catwalk in white leather.

'Oh, she's great,' says Mikel, 'but she won't travel. She only works in Paris. Now I want to play you some music. When I play this at the beginning, nothing will happen. Like the lights will go out on the catwalk or something, then the next bit comes on and three of the star people will come out and we'll fade into some other form of music like Tamla Motown or Marvin Gaye. So don't think it's very odd and that it's going to go through the whole of your first scene.'

'It obviously *is* very odd, or you wouldn't be giving me this big build up.'

'You might know it,' says Mikel, 'but I think it's so brilliant that if you don't want it I'm going to give it to someone else.'

Bruce and George chorus a camp 'Get you!'

'No, it *has* to open a show. Right . . .'

'AS LONG AS
IT DOESN'T
LOOK LIKE
A CUT-RATE
BARGAIN
BASEMENT
SHOW . . .'

He plays the opening bars of *The Kiss of the Spiderwoman*, sending waves of waltzing, yearning music washing over the room. Then William Hurt's voice is heard, intoning *'She's . . . well, she's something a little strange. That's what you notice . . . that she's not a woman like all the others.'*

'Have you seen it?'

'Yes,' says Bruce. 'It was *dreadful*.'

'It's a bit depressing,' says Mikel, disappointed. 'But the music isn't. What he's saying can go on while the models come out, then look at themselves in the mirror.'

'She seems all wrapped up in herself,' continues William Hurt. *'Lost in a world she carries deep inside her . . . surrounded by a world of luxury and sumptuousness. Her bed, all quilted satin, chiffon drapes . . . From her window she can see the Eiffel Tower.'*

Bruce raises his voice. 'I mean, he wasn't actually that good, although everyone raves about him. I really didn't like it.'

'This music is so pretty,' says Russell.

'But now, that man she's been waiting for all her life – a real man – is near. Her maid has prepared her a foaming bath . . . her toenails painted a rosy peach . . . she unfastens her taffeta nightgown . . .'

'How much of this are we supposed to have?'

'Oh, only the beginning, and then the waves of music and then cross-fade into the next. But I think we could return to that maybe once and at the end.'

'That would be great,' says Bruce. 'More champagne?' Mikel sits down, relieved. 'Now we've got to find about twelve other pieces.'

Russell takes over. 'I'll just put this on. You might hate it but it's new.' He plays a snatch of Jocelyn Brown's

Love's Gonna Get You, followed by French funk.

'This is new club music,' he says.

Bruce pulls an imaginary loo chain. Russell resorts to safer Grace Jones.

'How old is this?' asks Bruce. 'I think I've even got this one.'

'Well, this is a compilation,' says Russell.

'She's so arch,' says Bruce. 'It's all so technological and manufactured. I think you should record me over this, saying "I knew Grace Jones in Paris back in 1973 . . ." Or me saying "Grace *who*?"'

'We've got that tape of Bruce's *Desert Island Discs* – we should cut bits out of that and use them,' suggests Mikel. 'Why don't we use that whole tape, while people are coming in and waiting for the show to start? We'll use it like wallpaper music during the forty-five minutes it takes for the show to get started.' The idea pleases Bruce.

'Will we have to get permission?' asks George. 'It's BBC property.'

'We'd better,' agrees Bruce. 'Although they shouldn't mind. We're not selling it.'

'No, but don't forget it will be on the video too.'

'We'll deal with that,' says Bruce to Mikel. 'What's this?'

Russell has started to play a Jane Birkin album. She breathes a few words against a relentless low rhythm. *'Vie morte . . . et resurrection d'un amour passion . . . nous sommes foutu.'*

'It's nice,' says Bruce 'But is it dirty?' No one knows. He picks up the phone and dials. 'This is a French-speaking pal I'm ringing. Hallo darling. I'm listening to a dirty French song and she says *"Nous sommes foutu"*. Does that mean what I think it does?' He giggles. 'Oh, it means we're in trouble. OK darling, just checking. See you soon. Ciao. She says it depends on how it's used.'

'I think we've got almost the amount we need now,' says Mikel. 'We've got enough.'

'What have we got?' says Bruce. 'I've only heard three tracks I like!'

'We've got Jocelyn Brown, the French rude thing, Spiderwoman for several bits that we can link into other music, the Grace Jones . . .'

'I wouldn't mind losing Grace Jones, actually. You know the ideal fashion show is for me to be backstage completely hyped up, tearing my hair and screaming, but knowing this hell is only going to last twenty minutes, then also at the same time getting off on the music. What else? We aren't going to use any video tricks are we?'

'No! We've got mirrors, lighting and *mah*-vellous clothes.' Mikel laughs. 'We've got to order colour gels for you. What colours would you like?'

The gels colour the spotlights and charge the mood of a group of clothes in a collection. Clever use of gels can hype up the colours and make sequins glitter like stars.

'Brown, brown, brown! Can you get sepia?'

'It's difficult, but we can get it. What's the last scene? Grand? What colour's grand?'

'I've got all these really couture velvet and mink jobs, and black with gold. Very Vincent Price, you know? I slung in some red there and it did look rather fab, but it also had this *jolie dame*, Valentino look about it. So I thought, stick to chic, and black. I've got black and royal blue. Perhaps I could do more, it always looks better to send out a ton of the same thing, but when you get to that price range – £4,000 a frock . . .'

'And what about hair?'

'I've got thirty-two hats with ninety outfits. It's going to take a ridiculous amount of time to get the hats on.'

'Sassoon are very capable. And there are enough of them. Do you agree?'

'OK. I like this music – what is it?'

Russell is playing Mick Jagger and Tina Turner's Band Aid track.

Mikel starts putting albums back in their sleeves.

'I have to come to you early next week and go through the running order, then come back and do the final stage. Then the following week we'll come over the night before and label the clothes.'

Bruce puts back his head and warbles. 'It's coming clo–o–o–ser!'

'We'll put the models' fees down, then get the costings a little nearer and then add what you essentially need. We'll have to pay for the mirror and the set-up, but we won't go mad.'

'You don't have to feel guilty as long as we have a ballpark figure beforehand,' says Bruce. 'Just as long as it doesn't look like a cut-rate bargain basement show.'

PLANNING
THE
SHOW

FRANCINE SCHIFFER

MAKE-UP

On Friday 28 February Francine Schiffer – a slim, vivid brunette with spiky short hair – sits on a stool in Bruce's studio drinking coffee and making notes while Bruce informs her about his colours: brown, black and bright red; and his fabrics: leather, bronze lamé, crêpes and petrol-coloured sequins. He shows her a number of half-finished dresses. He's simultaneously dealing with a domestic crisis. At home, his bathwater has been leaking through the ceiling of the flat below, and he is arranging for an 8 a.m. appointment with the plumber.

Francine is a freelance make-up artist, and like many of the best in her profession she is affiliated to a cosmetic house, Charles of the Ritz. She has worked with Bruce for over four years. They are working out a striking new make-up for the show which will look right with every garment and every fabric, will key in with the colours and take into account the effects of lighting on the catwalk. 'I think we could do something fab with that mustardy gold,' says Francine. 'Possibly pale faces and dark eyebrows. We can get away from red lips and do something with bronze and brown.'

The discussion moves to models. Bruce will have seven black or half-caste models, ten brunettes and only one blonde. They talk about the lighting with its predominance of brown, red and gold gel filters, and hats, which will not hide the eyes as they are off the face. The hair will be by a team from Vidal Sassoon. Francine likes 'mad stuff' for the hair. Bruce doesn't. 'It's got to be sleek,' he tells her. 'I don't want the girls to look like idiots. It has to look thought through, and I've got lots of bobs anyway.'

They make an appointment and model booking for the test the following week. Francine sums up. 'What I'm seeing at the moment is loose gold powder dusted across the eyes up through the eyebrows, with burnished mustardy gold on the eyelids, very strong brown eyes, a brownish gold cheek and a strong brown lip. With that gold lighting, the metallic look will be read even from the back row.'

'Right. On the fifteenth the girls are arriving at 7.30. The show's at 12.25.'

'I'll have someone start foundation at 7.30, and I'll be there at 8.30 for when you have finished rehearsing.'

'Just don't forget that eighteen girls is a lot to get made up in the time available. And the starettes will arrive at the last minute. Marie and Pat are doing Jasper before me. If Jasper ends at 11.30 it should be all right.'

When Francine arrives for the second session on the following Thursday, 6 March, she walks into a crowded day. One of the house models, Jane, is being drawn in a number of Oldfield outfits for the *Daily Mail*. The *TV AM* crew are around: they film Jane, and Bruce at work in the workroom. The *Los Angeles Times* is also here, working on an article.

Francine looks quite different from last week's incarnation. She now has a three-foot pony tail, black and white make-up with scarlet lips and nails, and resembles an early Audrey Hepburn. She gets to work on model Anna Curtis in the strong light from the window. Bruce, in the background, is pinning and cutting away on a stand, shaping the intricately draped bodice of a flashing silver paillettes dress needed by Stefanie Powers on Tuesday for the big scene in a TV pilot she is in London to film. Work proceeds in the comparative silence of Radio 4.

Francine touches out any shadows on Anna's near-perfect complexion, applies a light foundation and

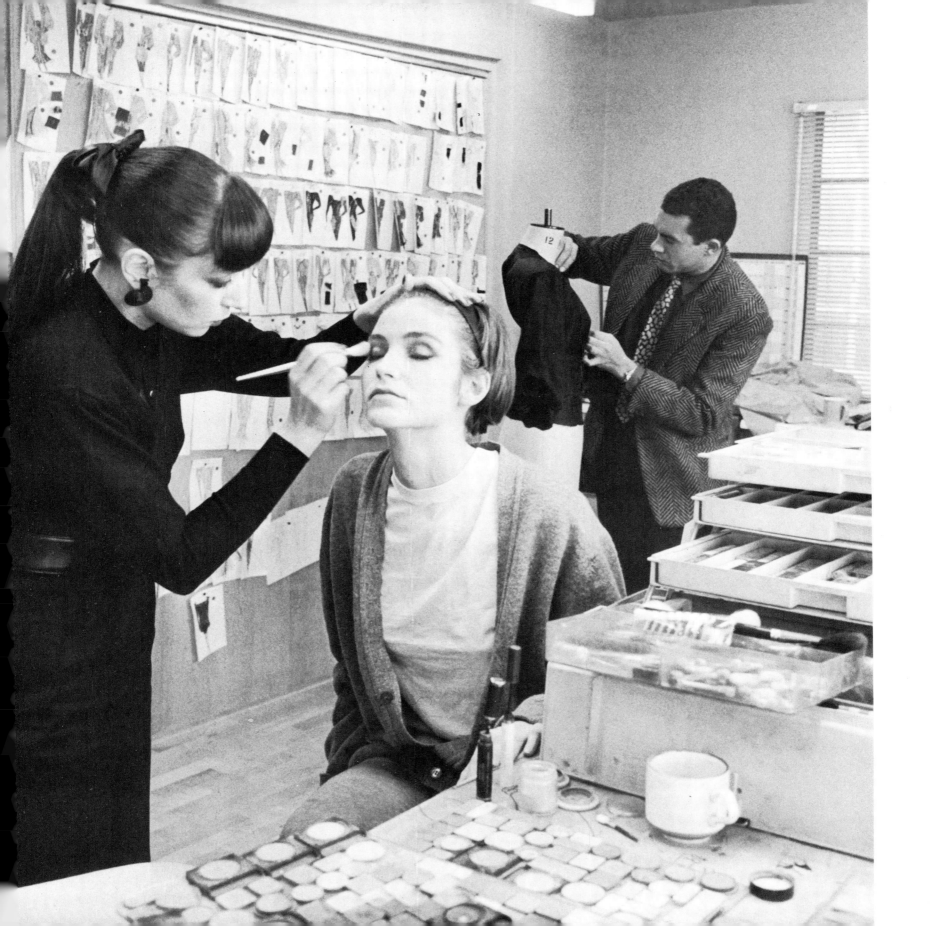

FRANCINE AT WORK:
'WITH THAT GOLD
LIGHTING, THE MET-
ALLIC LOOK WILL BE
READ EVEN FROM
THE BACK ROW'

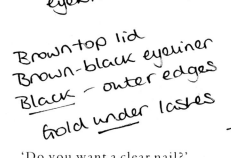

powder, and brushes mimosa-yellow and gold-dust powder across the zone of the face that would be covered by spectacles: upwards from the eyes through the eyebrows, and across the bridge of the nose. She touches the eyelashes with gold mascara, draws brown wings in to the eyes and applies bronze blusher to the cheeks. After twenty minutes she paints in brown lips and shows her work to Bruce.

'Nice,' he says. 'Will it show up clearly enough from the catwalk?'

'I think maybe it could be a bit stronger.' She works on for another ten minutes, developing the cat's eye outlines.

'I like that. It's better,' says Bruce.

'It's a strong, womanly make-up to go with your clothes,' says Francine. 'Now let's see it with one of your dresses.'

Anna slips into one of Bruce's jersey dresses, and walks up and down the studio. 'Great,' says Bruce. 'Don't change a thing.'

Francine writes in her leather diary:

Pale face
Gold brushed through eyebrows with gold mascara

Brown top lid
Brown-black eyeliner
Black – outer edges
Gold under lashes

Gold mascara lower lashes
Brownish cheeks
Brown lips

'Do you want a clear nail?'

'Just a clear nail.'

Francine draws a line under her notes. 'Meeting over.'

'IT'S A STRONG, WOMANLY MAKE-UP'

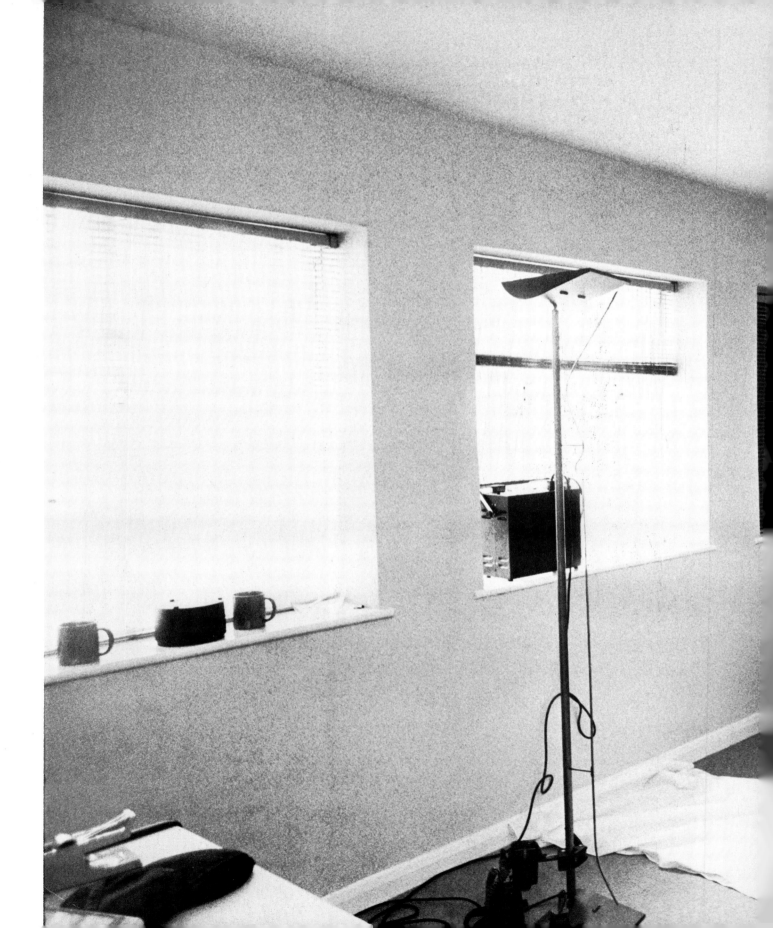

THE SHOOT FOR THE
LOS ANGELES TIMES.

PLANNING THE SHOW

ACCESSORIES

Carol Graves-Johnston's company is Cingula: she
manufactures belts from her home and workroom in
Stockwell, South London. Formerly a librarian at the
Courtauld Institute, she began to make belts in the
sixties, learning her skills over a six-year period with
expert belt-maker Kitty Pines. Cingula supplied
Belville Sassoon and Victor Edelstein before Carol was
invited to show her work to Bruce Oldfield. She designs
and makes the belts with Camilla Meade, her assistant,
putting specialised work out to casters and buckle-
makers such as Sarina de Majo and Andrew Lammas.
'Periodically I take in my latest designs to show Bruce.
He will pick some and make adaptations to suit his
clothes, so that in the end the belts have his own
particular handwriting. Sometimes he will ask me to take
a design further, make it up in a certain fabric he will
give me, or change the look in some way. He is very easy
to work with because he knows exactly what he wants.

TAFFETA BELTS AND

TURBANS

Taffetta
et 73.

cinched waist
ruched Taft
belt

Taft
Turban.

Lisa Vandy
Brogue Buckle

'When I take the second selection he places orders for the show. From an initial seven designs this time I made half a dozen of each, perhaps forty belts in all for the show. Usually there will be some last-minute additions when I deliver these about two days before the show. Belts are always the last thing to go into a collection, because you don't know exactly what is needed before the dress is made up. Then after the press and private customers' showings, when Bruce's orders come through, we edit the belts again, dropping one or two and making others for Bruce to sell separately as accessories in his shop.

'For this winter collection Bruce banished the hip belt and brought back the waist. One important shape was a wide black patent belt cut out over the hips so that it sat well and was comfortable to wear. We had a problem with one belt that twisted two colours and did up with two buckles. It looked great but it would have been no good for the show because it took too long to release. In the end I made it with fake buckles and easy fastenings underneath.

'If there is a problem with a belt, it is usually to do with the fastenings. We had to drop one belt because it had to be closed in Velcro, and if you sneezed it self-destructed. I made some variations on a knotted belt which did up by slotting a metal dagger through a complicated loop. It looked great, so Bruce asked me to take it over to the shop and show Marie and Neila how to knot it, so they could show the customers.'

THE BULLION MOTIF:
SHOES AND BERET

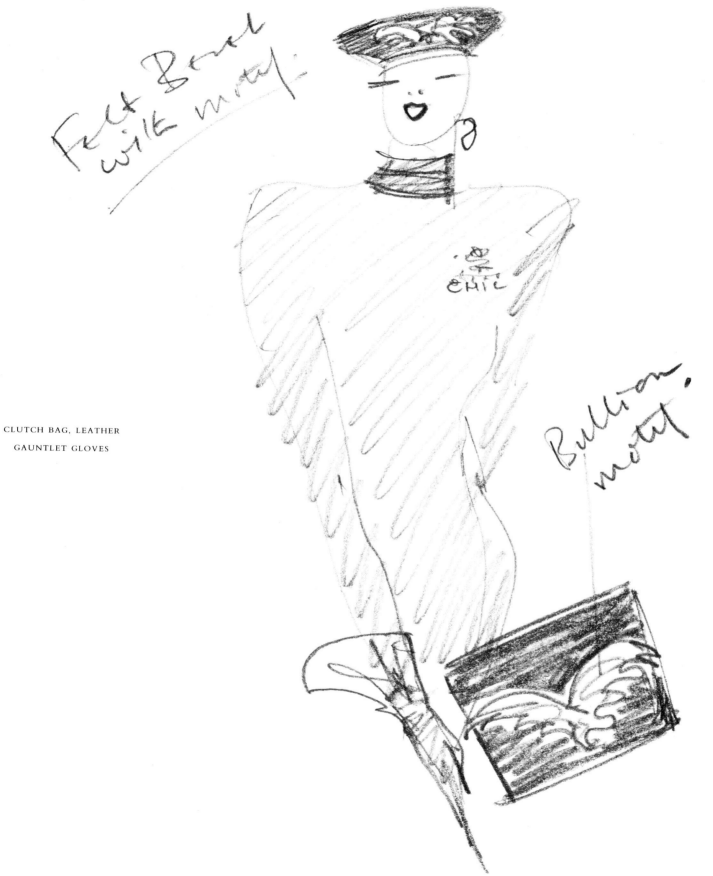

Felt Beret
with motif.

CHIC

Bullion
motif.

CLUTCH BAG, LEATHER
GAUNTLET GLOVES

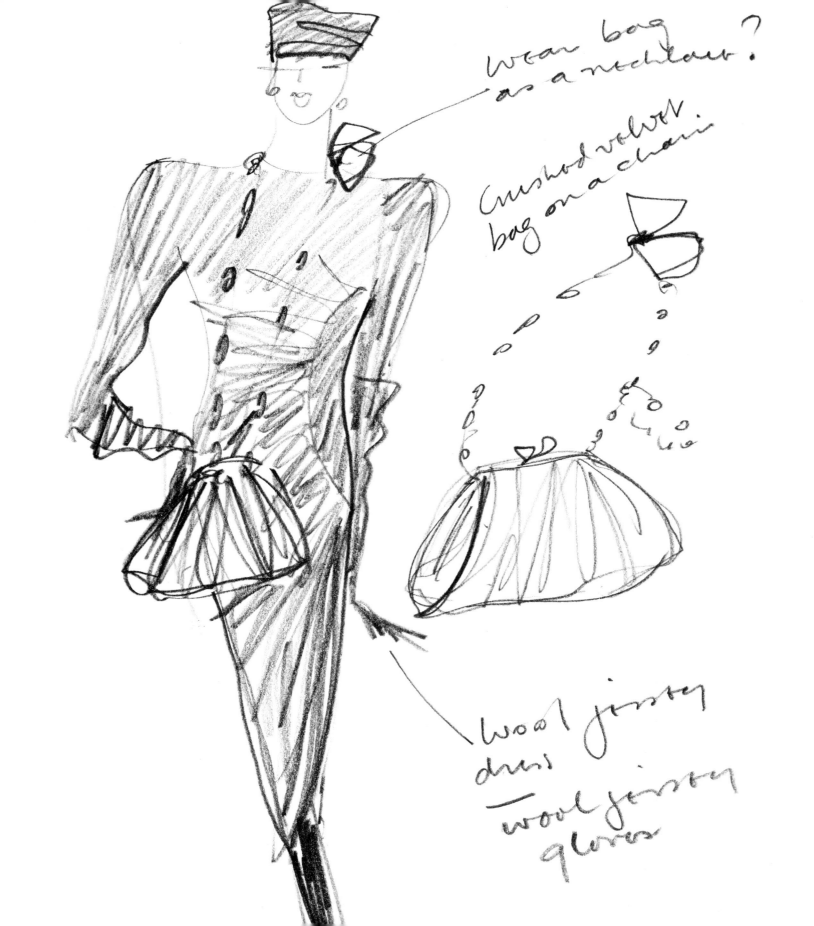

Big bow in
Taffeta at
top arm.

or wrist

Taff hat
v. romantic.
Big bow

Bow on
pony tail?

11

THE
WEEK
BEFORE

From Sunday 9 March, when Anita, Ros and George
sit down to finalise the invitations and seating plan
for the show, to Friday 14 March, when the office is
crammed with rails of labelled garments, the week
passes in an ever-accelerating rush. Fittings go on
day and night, at whatever time a garment reaches the
stage when it can be tried on the house model, Jane,
or the temporary model, Jackie. There are costings to be
done, ready for when orders are taken. There are
more preview photographs and interviews for press
and TV, accessorising to be completed, shoes to be
collected. Arrangements and times have to be confirmed
with the model agencies. Mikel Rosen and his team are
keeping track of the latest garments to be added or
dropped ready for the working-out of the final running
order on Friday. The last-minute sketches must be made
up into patterns and toiles and sent to the outworkers.
There are gloves, bags and leathers to be collected
from British Rail Red Star. Transport and insurance
have to be arranged for the garments on Saturday, to
arrive at Cadogan Hall, Duke of York Barracks, by
7 a.m. and afterwards to be sent on to the shop for the
buyers to see on Sunday. The furs must be accompanied
by a security guard from the moment they leave
Birger Christensen in New Bond Street on Friday
evening until they are returned there after the show
on Saturday afternoon.
As for the shop and the made-to-measure sales, this
week is like any other week of the year. Business does
not stop because it is collection time, and the
appointments and interruptions continue as usual.
Everyone is working to capacity and towards the
end of the week tempers get frayed.

MONDAY –
working off the nerves

For the second day running, Bruce can be found
sewing in the workroom before 9 a.m. The previous
day, Sunday, he worked from 8 a.m. to 8 p.m., letting
himself into the empty premises in Argon Mews to
cut out and machine five black dresses. 'I find cutting
and sewing therapeutic. It stops me thinking and
getting nervous.'

This new group of black dresses has been designed
specifically for the gold bullion ordered a month
previously from Bombay and finally received on
Friday. Strands of coiled gold wire threaded across
an appliqué shape and firmly padded, bullion was
originally devised for Moghul costume and for
maharajahs, but it is better known in Britain as the
'scrambled egg' on air marshals' caps and admirals'
jackets.

'When it arrived it was so sensational I decided to
design a new group of dresses for it,' Bruce explains
as he tacks the gold swags to a neckline. 'As we're so
short of time I want to see just how little stitching will
keep these on. Some of these dresses will be held
together by pins and a prayer! At this stage we have to
cut corners: they couldn't possibly go out as finished
production garments with sewing like this. We can
perfect the dresses later. Oddly enough, the last-
minute designs often turn out to be the best.'

BRUCE IN THE
WORKROOM: 'IT'S
THERAPEUTIC. IT
STOPS ME THINK-
ING AND GETTING
NERVOUS'

TUESDAY –
the seating headache

Ros Woolfson has had 209 requests for seats from the foreign press alone. Anita Richardson is trying to cut down on the buyers. 'Each store or company wants to send all members of staff who are over here. Saks Fifth Avenue, for instance, wanted twenty-six seats. They got seven. Then there are Seibu and Isetan from Japan, and the Europeans. We check it out with our agents. You can work the seating two ways. Either you put the buyers you like in the good seats, or the ones who buy most. I tend to do the latter. For instance, Bloomingdales bought well last season, so I have given them three front-row seats.'

Numbering the tickets from the seating chart drawn up by Tony Askew, whose firm will be supplying the chairs and lighting for Cadogan Hall, Duke of York Barracks, on Saturday and Sunday, Ros and Anita sent out the final invitations yesterday. This morning, there is a call from Tony Askew's firm to say there has been a mistake over the number of seats: they will have to manage with ninety fewer chairs. Ros and George immediately go off in a taxi to see the problem for themselves. By shortening the catwalk and bringing in three extra rows of chairs at the foot of the hall, Ros manages to fit in an extra seventy seats. 'Now if we tell the workroom they have to stand at the back we're almost back to 400,' she says.

'EXCUSE ME JACKIE,
I'M NOT TAKING
LIBERTIES . . .'

WEDNESDAY – *fittings.*
Ironing out the problems

Bruce is frowning at a brown silk dress with a drape
front being worn by Jackie, the extra house model.
Judith stands by, with scissors and pins.
'Excuse me, Jackie. I'm not taking liberties. I'm just
putting my hand up your skirt.' Bent double, he turns to
Judith. 'There's something funny about the hem, but
don't disturb the whole of the skirt to do it. Give it a
good press and forget it. We'll get it right in
production.'
Ros puts her head round the door. 'Won't keep you.
Just to say that I've fixed you up for a 2.30 press
interview. I've told them ten minutes only. And
Canadian Television at 4.30.'
'Fine! But they'll have to take me as they find me.'
Jackie reappears in a narrow furl of black crêpe, long-
sleeved and covered up to the neck. When she turns the
cape back flies open and reveals a backless plunge.
'This is a winner!' says Bruce. 'It feels right.
Any age or type can wear it.'
'Yes – it's such a lovely back and so firm on the
shoulder,' Judith agrees.
'It's great. Not one wrinkle. Judith – it's bloody good.'
The next dress, a short red sheath of silky jersey with a
swag falling asymmetrically from hip to thigh,
presents problems. Bruce unpicks the swag. 'We need
to run off a bit more on the fall, and taper the skirt.
All these patterns need a little extra on the hips. And we
need red topstitching on the top and bottom of the skirt.'
Jane now comes in wearing a dress of peacock chiffon.
The torso is wrapped round with two diagonally

slanting swathes of beading: the skirt flares out gently
from below the second band.

Anita looks over the model's shoulder at Bruce.

'I'm upping the insurance in the shop. There were two
boutique burglaries last night in Sloane Street and
Hans Crescent, and that's very close to home.'

Bruce nods and wrestles with the beaded band. 'This is
wrong,' he says. 'I don't like the way it broadens on the
shoulder. It's £400-worth of embroidery, and it's
wrong.'

George comes in to bring the sketch board up to date.
Blue and red dots indicate which design is docketed
to the workroom and which to an outworker. A green
star marks designs with all pieces complete, a gold star
means the garment is finished and hanging on the rail.

Jackie returns, modelling a glittering black polo-neck
dress, mini length. 'Is this right, Bruce?'

'Oh yes. Will you ask Lynne for the purple chiffon
petticoat she has on the stand?'

The full, filmy skirt goes underneath the dress. Bruce
picks a length of matching purple taffeta off
the floor and ties an enormous bow round one wrist.
Suddenly the whole outfit comes together. Jackie, with
her platinum crop, looks like a reincarnation of a fifties
Vogue cover.

'Sort of delicious, no?'

Bruce calls in a junior. 'Katy, this is your job. Get one-
inch elastic, make a casing so it's like a silk garter. The
bow goes on that. It's going to have to be bagged out
and stitched up here. You'll get it out of a width. Cut
it on the bias – but remember, bias seams can stretch,
so take care!'

'SORT OF DELICIOUS, NO?'

GEORGE UPDATES
THE SKETCHBOARD

THURSDAY –
costing God's creations

Some fifty garments fill the rails, almost every one pinned with a sheet headed 'From the Desk of God' – a Christmas present from Anita to Bruce – printed with terse orders.

'Topstitch round panel'
'Good press'
'Style tag. Button at waist and cuffs'
'Check bodice'
'B/holes'

Bruce sidesteps Helen from the workroom, who is taking away three outfits to finish. 'And for God's sake use a damp cloth,' he calls after her. 'Those seams are shiny!' He is carrying a khaki and gold winged dress already photographed by the *New York Times,* the *Telegraph* and the Silk Commission. 'Do you know what?' he says to George. 'These wings are on *upside down.*'

The video is on in Bruce's studio: his voice can be heard behind an Italian translation, saying, 'The Princess of Wales has increased the prestige of British fashion now. The British hate blowing their own trumpet – she does it for them.'

Barry, Bruce's foster brother, raffish in a leather blouson, has dropped in to use the word processor. 'Somebody', says Bruce meaningfully, 'is using this place as his *office.*' Barry, five feet six inches, ogles the five feet ten inch Jane.

'She's too big for you,' Bruce tells him fraternally.

'Oh no. I can handle it.'

Meanwhile, in the workroom, Christine is preparing the costings and Lynne is checking them: the wholesale prices must be completed for the first post-show business with the buyers. For each style the paper pieces are fitted jigsaw-pattern on to the fabric as economically as possible, and the metreage noted on the costing sheet.

'If we make one of these dresses it will take 3.40 metres, but if we cut two together we can do it in 6 metres, saving 80 centimetres over two garments,' explains Christine. 'We cost on an average, because we sometimes make up to 100 garments of a style. The finished costings also take account of time and hand finishing.' The magnificent medieval velvet being stitched by Emilia to a mink collar for the grand finale will be enormously expensive because, with its built-in boned foundation fastened like a corset with a row of tiny hooks and eyes, and its great sweep of fabric, it has taken forty-five hours to make.

In the office, George is making her sixth call to a model agency, chasing girls who haven't turned up yet to try on their dresses. 'It has *got* to be tomorrow,' she is saying. 'It's the only day left.'

12

FRIDAY . . .

the day before the show . . .

MORNING

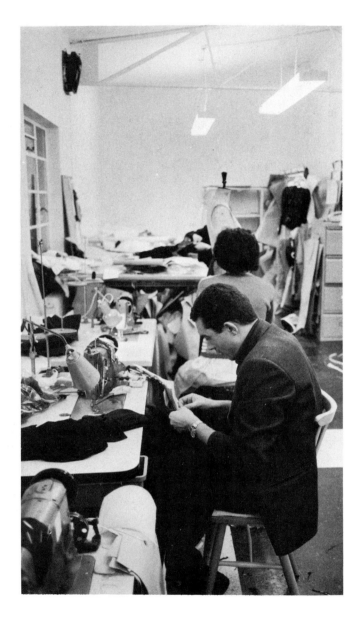

Bruce, who worked until 10 p.m. the previous night, is in at 8 a.m. and finds George taping the soles of forty-two pairs of shoes for the show, to protect them against scratching. The shoes had to be bought, but in the end the price was below wholesale cost. Simple, black high-heeled leather and grosgrain evening shoes, they have been picked to suit everything on the catwalk. Bruce sits straight down at a machine and gets to work on a lamé tunic. He has taken the place of a machinist who had a tiff with her neighbour in the workroom, walked out at lunchtime yesterday and hasn't been seen since.

The studio and workroom are choked with garments, and open boxes everywhere spill out hats, gloves and jewellery. On a shelf lies a jumble of sample left shoes, Bruce's special shoe collection for Rayne: having reached the presentation stage, the left shoes have come here to be displayed in his showroom while the right ones are on show to buyers in Bond Street.

Mignon from Mikel Rosen's office arrives to work out the running order of the dresses and groupings for tomorrow: with her long curling hair, blooming rosy face, tartan sailor coat and button boots she looks like a child from a Victorian Christmas card. First, Mignon and George have to decide which girl shall wear which dress. Many models are too thin for plunging necklines, others don't look good in trousers. Mignon has to place two groups which will appear alternately on the catwalk giving time for the girls to change. The sketches on the board are up to date, and the daytime outfits are sorted into leathers, crêpes topstitched with bugle beads, suits in combinations of poison green and black diamond weaves, jerseys, crushed velvets and silk prints. George takes down the first group of sketches and Mignon checks to see whether they are all completed and on the rails. Today the remaining thirty-two outfits will come through from outworkers and the workroom. Mignon takes a great sheaf of papers out of her bag. They are the models' names to pin to each outfit for tomorrow.

'There are meant to be nine outfits in this leather section, but there are only six,' says Mignon.

'That's because we've scrubbed the gold section. Now we've put the two blonde leathers with the gold tweeds and the pleated lurex. And the leather man rang us to say they couldn't finish the last leather suit in time.'

'All right, so what do you consider the most amazing outfit for this part? You know the way Mikel works. It's got to begin very important and dramatic. Pat should wear this. She's got absolutely nothing up top but it won't matter. She will be able to carry it off.' She fills in her running sheet. 'Pat on her own. Then Hazel and Dina together, Janelle last. We'll save Marie for next.' George is pinning the names on to the garments. 'Where are the leather pants for this?' she wonders.

Mignon unpins the next group of sketches.

'I need to know who's wearing a skirt and who's wearing pants. I haven't seen Annette yet – what's she like?'

'She hasn't come in: she's from Kevin Arpino.'

'So she'll be good. Ivonska's brill, Tarita's brill. What colour hair is Ivonska? Because Michelle is Chinese-looking. Then Jane and Amanda. Which is the more masculine-looking of the two? We'll put her in pants.'

Angus, the stock manager, appears with the missing

OCCASIONALLY THERE'S A MURMUR – 'IT'S SUMMER OUT THERE. HAVE YOU NOTICED?'

165

leather pants.

'You are the hero of the day,' George tells him, hanging them up.

Meanwhile, an ironing and pressing professional has arrived, a large, poker-faced woman who is uncharmed by Bruce's enthusiastic greeting. 'It's that sort of thing,' says Bruce, waving to the rail. She doesn't move a muscle.

Bruce does a little dance. 'Would you like to see the pressing equipment?'

'I've seen it,' she says. 'It's not what I'm used to.'

'The way I got you,' says Bruce expansively, 'is I asked for a really great presser. The best.'

'I don't know about that equipment.'

'It's a great help,' says Bruce. 'It's a great help having you here anyway.'

She is led off to the steam room. Bruce mimes tearing his hair out, and runs back to the workroom.

Mignon is looking at a group of Aztec prints on the rail. 'This is going to go short short long short short. We'll have three coming on together in the middle, a black girl in the centre. This dress looks dumb here. It belongs in another group. Or can we take it out?'

'You can't leave out the jerseys, because that's what they like. We could move it in with these.'

Judith comes in, reads the latest notes from God, and takes four garments away.

'Now the next thing I want to ask you', Mignon says, 'is how many have you got in the diamond tweed section? It looks like ten, and I've only got eight girls available.'

Anita catches up with Bruce on the landing.

'Has anyone asked you about the furs being used in the show at the Savoy on Sunday? Do you have any objections?' The show will exhibit the highlights of all the collections from London Fashion Week.

'It limits me,' Bruce says. 'I'm going on with one person, showing one dress, Anna Harvey, the fashion editor from *Vogue*. I don't want the dress covered up.'

'All right, I'll tell them.'

Bruce runs through to the office. 'Can you hurry up and put the labels on, please?'

A drained-looking model with dark circles under her eyes comes in wearing three dirty sweaters and starts checking on the labels to see what she has to wear tomorrow.

Bruce makes a call to Diane Hall, his design assistant at the shop, who takes the fittings when he cannot be there.

'You know that dress on loan to Stefanie Powers that we made on Tuesday? Well, it was too tight for her. They filmed her, but they had to cheat. She kept popping out all over the place. Well, she's got to wear it again for the BAFTA Awards on Sunday. Obviously I

GEORGE AND MIGNON PONDER THE RUNNING ORDER

CHRISTINE WITH THE LATEST DESPATCH FROM GOD

haven't got time to fit her. So what we have to do is go over to the hotel . . . Oh *thank you*, darling, can you? It's a pain in the neck, that fabric. No way can we alter it properly in time. It's got a ruched midriff, but you can't actually ruche that fabric, so it was cut away, laid over and stitched down, piece by piece. We've got to put a panel down the centre of the back and hide it under the middle of a bow. We can't do it properly, but it will look good as long as no one looks inside it!'

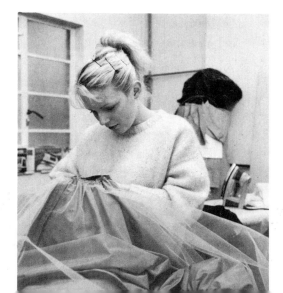

AFTERNOON

'Where's his lordship?' someone asks.

'Machining next door.'

In the workroom Radio 2 plays. Judith comes
in and out, making tiny finishing details on each
garment. Occasionally there's a murmur from the
machinists. 'It's summer out there,' they say to each
other. 'Have you noticed?' Or 'This client needs to
diet.'

Outside there is a thundering noise. Christine running
upstairs and Judith running downstairs have collided
over a mound of taffeta crinoline. Judith begins
burrowing under the hem. 'What rubbish have they put
under there?' 'You name it,' Christine says, 'it's there.'
Mignon and George are still labouring over the running
order when a van comes into the yard. The furs have
arrived. The security guard sitting in Anita's office
helps unload them while Anita fastens and double-locks
the metal grilles over the windows. Picking her way
round the cars and unloading bay, a coffee-coloured
beauty in a suede coat waves up to George.

'Bruce!' calls George. 'Hazel's here if you want to say
hullo.'

Hazel Collins, sister-in-law to Joan, is one of the
celebrity models who will be showing Bruce's clothes
tomorrow. An old friend of Bruce and Anita, she is a
property developer and owns a hairdressing salon in
Walton Street.

'Hullo, darlings,' she greets them. 'Listen, I've been on
a Get Fat diet. I've got tits now.' She sticks them out.
'Get me!'

TINY FINISHING DETAILS

At 4 p.m. there's a phone call from Pat Cleveland's
agent in London. George, noticeably paler, turns to
Bruce.
'Pat isn't coming. Her baby's ill. She has to stay in New
York.'
There is a moment's silence before Bruce shrugs. 'What
can I do? I'm past caring.'
'They've got a substitute, Linda Spering: she's in
London now.'
Bruce says nothing.
George says, 'OK, let's see her,' and puts the phone
down. She goes to make a comforting cup of tea for the
two of them.

. . . AND EVENING

It is now late in the evening, and everyone has just
finished eating the pizzas that Bruce has had brought in.
Back to work.

In the workroom Marcia is talking to her sister on the
telephone.

'No, I won't be back yet. Yes, I've had a pizza. You
have? Well, give it to the dog.'

George is writing a poster-size notice on the board
which says:

Van   Ironing board   Irons   Clothes   Publicity material
Van sticker for car park   Seating plan   Shoe sizes list

Christine has noticed that there are no buttons on a
gold blouse and offers to sew some on, but there are
none suitable. She sits on the floor covering metal
buttons with scraps of lamé. Anita almost trips over her
as she comes in to say, 'I've never seen Marcia looking
so exhausted. George, have you got the fur prices?'

Bruce will be using pieces from a number of jewellers
in the show, and now Lisa Vandy arrives with her
selection. 'Sorry I'm late,' she says. 'Things have been
frantic. My own deadline is Monday. I've an
appointment for 9 a.m. with the Bloomingdales buyer
and I've got to sort out my costings before then.'

Bruce begins checking through what she's brought in,
metal and silver pieces which she makes, finishes and
polishes by hand.

'Are you going to manufacture any of this stuff?' he says.
'Ask me another time.'

George starts packing belts, gloves and shoes into
boxes, and boxes into crates, tying the bottoms of
polythene dress bags and bagging the lamés. Christine
gets up stiffly from the floor. 'I'm off,' she says. She still
has to pick up two last garments from the outworkers
and deliver them to Chelsea Barracks early tomorrow
morning, as they will have missed the van.

Bruce snaps up a junior who has looked in inquiringly,
hoping to be allowed to go. 'Can you
cope with doing me a pin hem? And these two
leather jackets need a second button.'

Then he hides his face in his hands. 'Let me just run
through and see if there's anything else. Because
the things have to be in the van at 6.45 a.m. tomorrow.
Lynn, pad these velvet sleeves with lots of tissue.
They're supposed to be really fat. George, don't let
the model take it all out when she gets into the dress.
We can fill it out with crin later.'

George unexpectedly collapses on to the floor. She's
been on her feet since 7 a.m. It is now 1.05 a.m., and
eleven people are still working.

'I'm knackered,' Bruce says, suddenly. 'My back is
aching. I can't be bothered to do any more . . . You
visualise it all early on and you have to be fairly sure it
will work. Then when they're finished they don't
look so good as you'd originally planned. At this stage,
it's details, and making sure the groups look right
together.'

The priority now is to get everyone safely home: cabs
are booked and a few last-minute tasks are done
before the taxis arrive. Bruce has the final flicker of an
idea: he puts a textured black leather jacket with a
greige silk waistcoat blouse, shrugs, and puts on his
own jacket. He, Anita and George are the last to leave.
Downstairs he leans against the furs in Anita's office.
'Are we locking these into the stockroom overnight?'
'It wouldn't hurt.'

That done, they're on their way out. 'Goodnight,'
Bruce says to the security guard. 'Did you get some
pizza? See you tomorrow.'

Van
~~Ironing Board~~
Irons
Clothes ✳
Publicity material
Van Sticker for
Car Park.
Seating plan
Shoes sizes-
list

1.00 A.M.

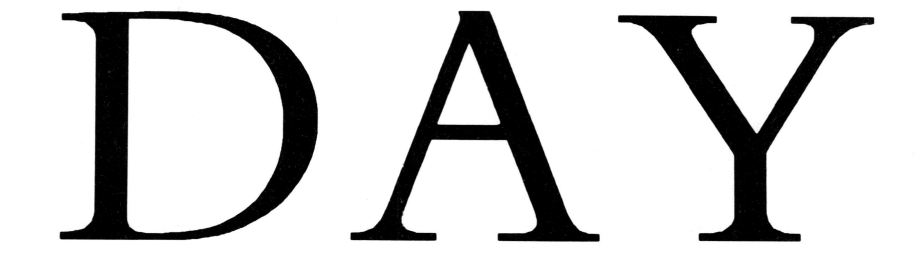

SATURDAY
15 MARCH
AT CADOGAN HALL,
DUKE OF YORK BARRACKS,
CHELSEA

6 A.M.: THE WORK-ROOM . . .

. . . AND CADOGAN HALL

It is 7 a.m. when Bruce's gold BMW cruises through the gates of Chelsea Barracks. An icy wind whips the tarmac and the watery sun highlights a line of soldiers climbing into an army lorry, one of them loitering to talk to a spike-headed girl in a floor-length coat and flat boots.

Back in Fulham, Anita, George and Keith, the guard, have begun loading the van with furs. On the catwalk in Cadogan Hall Bruce joins Mikel, Russell and Mignon.

'I didn't think you would be here until 9.00,' Mikel says.

'I couldn't sleep, after all,' Bruce admits.

They survey the prospect: a bleak brick shoe-box like a NAAFI, with metal-frame windows half concealed behind cheap black drapes, the T-shaped runway parting a sea of chairs. Mikel glares at a technician up a ladder.

'Those lighting engineers should have finished with the spotlights yesterday,' he says loudly. 'The other day, they were still working on the lighting at 2.30 and the Artwork show was supposed to begin at 3.30.'

The loudspeaker comes on with a bang and a blast of rock music. In the dressing-room, four steps down from the screened entrance to the catwalk, a band of T-shirted teenagers appear. They are the dressers, all students from St Martin's, shepherded by Ruth Stacey of the Joan Chapman Wardrobe Agency. For the next five hours they will be responsible for hanging up the clothes, getting the models in and out of them, and making sure the outfits appear in the correct order and with the right accessories. Mignon allots to each dresser the names of two models and hands out the running-order sheets.

Bruce does a tour of inspection.

'God knows how eighteen models and their dressers are all going to fit in here. Ninety-eight outfits, five changes each and this dressing-room can't be more than six feet by twenty-four. And there's nowhere for me to take a sneaky look out front.'

'You'll have the video immediately afterwards,' Mikel says.

The show is scheduled for noon. At 8.30 the van arrives and all hands start to unload. As the named clothes come through to the dressing-room, Mignon hands them out.

'Right, girls, have you all got rails? First outfit, Jane Spencer.'

George, staggering past with an ironing board, deftly fields two straying models and packs them off down the passage to the kitchens, where Francine and her assistants have spread out their make-up over the ovens and are beginning to apply foundation and gloss fingernails. Suddenly there are crowds of people jamming the entrance and the dressing-room. Ruth Stacey pushes in, shouting, 'I have a problem!' but no one is listening. She grips Bruce's arm. 'There's a model without a pass at the gate. They won't let her through because they haven't got her on the list. Who's got the list?' Bruce detaches his arm. 'Ask George.' The loudspeaker is at full volume again. Mikel's voice thunders 'MIGNON!' The uproar ceases. 'Yes?' calls Mignon, demurely.

'Um . . . aah . . . just testing.'

Out front, Mikel and the lighting manager go through the music and the spotlight changes: the manager writes down the colours on his running sheet. 'OK,' booms Mikel's expanded voice. 'Start mixing! There are five models coming down the runway. We want a thin

LOADING THE VAN

THE DRESSERS

A HAIRDRESSER CHECKS WITH BRUCE

SOUND AND LIGHTING TECHNICIANS

ANITA WITH THE BBC

LIGHTING

'GOD KNOWS HOW
WE'LL FIT IN HERE'

ACCESSORIES MATCHED TO CLOTHES

MODELS

yellow light on them. Now another group of girls is
emerging out of the back wall. Follow spots on the
second group, now! Big white light! This will be Marie
Helvin, out on her own.'

Bruce is trying to find the box of pillbox hats. To add
to the noise, two men with panels of sheet mirror are
hammering them to the screens that back the catwalk.
There are about 100 people in the hall now. George
pushes her way through to Bruce. 'You aren't going to
like this. There's a brigadier in the entrance, and he's
asking for tickets to the show. He's the organiser, so I
said I would have to find out.'

The brigadier is intrigued to meet Bruce.

'I saw you on breakfast TV. What's she like?'

'Who?'

'The blonde.'

'Selina? She's great.'

'You ought to give her some advice. She wears the
wrong colours.'

'Oh. Ah. As a matter of fact, she wears Bruce
Oldfield.'

'Could I be impertinent? My wife and I and our
daughter, we would like to see your show. My daughter
can stand.'

'I should think you'll all have to stand! All the seats are
numbered. But, as you're the boss . . . yes. But don't
go and tell me I've got too many people for the fire
regulations! Your name will be on the door.' Bruce looks
out of the corner of his eye at Frank and Guy, who have
arrived with a posse of hairdressers from Vidal
Sassoon. 'I've got to have a word with someone. See
you!'

A blast of Diana Ross drowns all voices except that of a
model who stands on the dressing-room steps and

shouts, 'Who's got me little brush?'

A dresser doubtfully regards a cutaway lurex tunic.

'Doesn't she have anything under this?'

'Just a bit of Blu-tack,' says George.

Bruce, pushing through with hats to show the hairdressers, reaches over her head and turns the hanger around.

'Oh, it's like *that*! Sorry!'

In the back kitchen, half the models have their foundation on and are greeting the hairdressers. Frank and Guy kiss them and stroke their hair, lifting it between thumb and forefinger as though it were fabric of a dubious quality. There is coffee in paper cups, and sticky buns in a box.

Bruce has found the belts and calls the dressers around him.

'They go round like this and tie centre front. Who's a girl guide? It should be a reef knot. You're really going to have to pull, girls, because they only look good when they are tight.'

Anita has escaped the mounting pressure of Cadogan Hall for the peace of Bruce's car. Locked in, she sits there with costings and a price list, working out the wholesale prices for the American buyers.

Meanwhile, inside the Hall, Mikel is ploughing through the second half of the lighting run-through.

'Bright light about now. Great! Next scene, four girls, two each side. Blue light! What's happening? Is something wrong?'

A cable has been left touching a light bulb and has burnt through. 'A general worker, please!' the cry goes up.

'A general worker to the floor!'

Russell appears with his headphones. 'There are five girls available. Do you want to rehearse?'

'All right. We'll get back to the lights. Can we do this scene *now* please. Tarita, will you stand in for Marie? We all need to move a bit quicker. We've only got one and a half hours and you all know I want to do quite a bit of rehearsal on this.'

Bruce is checking rails, taking a pair of pants from one, adding them to another outfit, scooping a camisole out of a dresser's hand and putting it with its skirt on the other side of the dressing-room. Ruth Stacey sits on a step, calmly sewing on a cuff button. 'It's the wrong button,' says George. 'It doesn't matter, dear. It won't show,' comes the reply.

'Where are the tights?' George asks Bruce.

'Where are the red sequin tops?' Bruce responds. 'And what, exactly, is this?' Pausing by a clothes rail, he points to a very old anorak hanging between crushed velvet and a waterfall of fiery sequins.

The dresser giggles. 'Don't be rotten. That's me windcheater.'

Mikel, meanwhile, is having a bad time.

'Third model, out now! Next! *Next!* NEXT! This is the wrong music. Stop the music, please. Can we hear the wallpaper music? Excuse me, you have the wrong side of the tape. We want the *Desert Island Discs* side. Please rewind. REWIND! Play it. Are you going to make a note? If the tape runs out as it will before the start of the show, rewind and play it from the beginning. You've come on in the goddamn middle.'

Russell and Mignon are talking earnestly to Bruce. Two of the expected models haven't arrived, and it is time they were made up. The first show this Saturday, John Rocha, has just ended in Tent Two, so they intend to go over there and find a couple of girls who aren't needed for the second show, Jasper Conran's. The

'LIKE A RUGGER SCRUM'

JUST BEFORE REHEARSAL

MIGNON

'THE PEACE OF BRUCE'S CAR'

IN THE KITCHENS: HAIR . . .

MIKEL CHANGES THE
RUNNING ORDER

MARIE

. . . AND MAKE-UP

PRESS

incident leaves Bruce nervous. 'We've got time,' he says to himself. 'It's still early.' Fighting his way across the dressing-room he suddenly loses his temper. 'Do you know what I want? Will you all get out of here for half an hour, please! Every time I move I'm falling over someone. It's a lovely day outside, so go for a walk.'

His voice can be heard all the way down to the kitchens, where the last relay of models are having their make-up finished. Two girls are doing yoga topless, watched with sidelong interest by Keith, the security man.

'This is the worst time for everybody,' says Kevin, Anita's husband, who has brought over a last-minute blouse from an outworker. 'No matter what you've done in the past or what happens after the show, at the moment it's all down to Bruce and he'll be judged by what happens now. He'll be all right tonight.'

Champagne is being served by Pat, the tea lady, who has come over from Fulham in her best dress. With the first pop of a cork Barry appears, straw hat balanced on the back of his head, thumbs stuck inside his braces.

'What are you doing, you rascal?' Kevin says.

'I heard there was a job going,' says Barry, 'helping the models get undressed.'

George puts Kevin's blouse with a leather jacket. 'There's a crowd outside,' Kevin tells her. 'Shirley Bassey's out there, with a minder.'

At 12.10 Mikel is still rehearsing, while Ros checks the seating numbers. At 12.20 the hall is cleared and she can unbolt the doors and let the audience in. Jasper Conran's show has ended late, in any case, and most of the crowd are still streaming across the quadrangle from Tent One. Cadogan Hall is now in velvety darkness, metal-frame windows and cheap drapery

invisible. A brilliant laser beam of light picks out the letters BRUCE OLDFIELD above the mirrored screen. Bruce's recorded voice from the BBC *Desert Island Discs* tape is intoning, 'I like crisp, quiet, gentle music. I've chosen a piece from Warlock's *Capriole Suite*.' Behind the scenes the returned dressers are helping the models into their first outfits. In the kitchen Mignon is standing on a chair.

'The second you've had your hair and make-up done can you get into your clothes, please. We're supposed to start in ten minutes.'

Russell, a somnambulist in headphones, is communicating with Mikel who sits at the mixing desk at the far end of the hall, watching the scene from the audience's point of view.

Marie Helvin has quietly slipped in from Jasper Conran's show and is half into Bruce's cream leather suit. In the kitchen, Mignon cannot make herself heard. Kevin puts down his glass and produces a table-rattling baritone. *'The show is going to start in five minutes.'*

In fact, it is 1.15 before the first models are collected at the foot of the steps in the dressing-room. Bruce is pulling belts tighter, adjusting the chains of shoulder bags and making last-minute changes to the jewellery. Russell motions to the entrance positions to left and right of the screen and stands, hand raised, ready for Mikel's 'Let's go!' The dressing-room has at last gone quiet. All noise ceases, and a voice announces, 'Ladies and gentlemen, please note that the fire exits are situated to the rear of the hall on the left hand side and at the front of the stage on the right. Please keep the gangways clear and refrain from smoking during the show. Thank you very much.'

BRUCE OLDFIELD

autumn/winter
collection

Now the *Kiss of the Spiderwoman* music spills into the hall and William Hurt's voice begins.

'She's, umm . . . well, she's something a little strange. The thing you notice, she's not a woman like all the others . . .' On go the girls for the first scene, drifting uncertainly, dreamily, following Mikel's choreography, the slow motion giving the audience time to take in the messages:

Bruce Oldfield means luxury,

Bruce Oldfield does furs,

Bruce Oldfield does leather . . .

There is a ripple of applause.

Once backstage, the slow motion ends abruptly. Whispers take the place of earlier shouts as returning models half run, half fall down the steps, pulling off their clothes as they go. Marie has her suit off before she's back by her rail, dropping jacket and blouse into a sea of hands. Bruce pushes evening gloves up the arms of a model who is having her hair combed and her necklace fastened. A model, still chatting *sotto voce*, is grabbed by the shoulders and physically propelled on to the stage.

Twenty-seven people in the dressing-room struggle and sway like a rugger scrum; and there is little light, because anything strong would show through on to the runway. There are clothes and belts and hats everywhere. Bruce's recorded voice booms out across Diana Ross' *Reflections*. 'I try to bring out the good points . . . one aims to flatter.' On the catwalk, bugle beading glitters, the red and black drape jerseys fill the stage like flags.

Marie, at every entrance, draws the applause as no other model here today can. On wave after wave of strong beat groups of beautiful black girls float down the runway in gold tweeds and leathers. Mignon and Russell, behind the screen, are literally dragging the girls up the steps and throwing them on to the stage. Tides of petrol-dipped sequins and winged gilded evening dresses wash across the mirror screens, and bursts of applause drown the music.

At 1.30, with eighty outfits down and eighteen to go, it is time for the finale. On they come, rank on rank of colour and sparkle, printed silks, black columns gilded with bullion, floating blues and sequins and fabulous medieval velvets with mink collars. As the clapping rises to a crescendo Marie pulls Bruce on to the stage and the models cluster round him, ululating and blowing kisses. Bruce's face is split in a wide grin. The audience rushes forward, and backstage and frontstage flow together like multi-coloured water.

When Bruce arrives backstage, another crate of champagne is being opened in the kitchens. One arm round his foster sister, Linda, he raises a glass to the models, still pulling on boots and thick sweaters. 'Thanks, girls!'

George alone doesn't join in the celebrations. She has
already sent the furs with Keith back to Birger
Christensen. Now she is loading the clothes on to the
van for Beauchamp Place. George and Anita will
organise the clothes into groups, ready for the buyers
tomorrow. For Ros, too, work is still in progress. She
steers Bruce towards his open-air interviews, round
the tarmac to the exit where the audience are pouring
out, filling him in as she goes. 'There's Junko Ouchi
from Japanese television, Jane Lomas from Pebble
Mill and Elsa Klench from Cable News Network.'
The Japanese film crew are set up and manage to film
Shirley Bassey in turban and Oldfield suit rushing
forward to kiss Bruce. 'Darling, that was wonderful! I
can't wait to try them all on! See you in the shop next
week.'

Ms Ouchi, all fringe and baggy linen jacket, comes
straight to the point.

'What has Princess Diana chosen for her Japanese trip?'

'Haven't you been briefed?' says Bruce to the camera.
'That's something I can't discuss. You saw a few
things on the runway, actually, but I can't tell you
which.'

'Congratulations on your show. Were you satisfied
with it?'

'Ninety-eight outfits in twenty minutes? I'll never do
it again!'

'And your future plans?'

'I would like to open shops, and I'm planning to get to
Japan before the end of the year.'

'You will definitely do business in Japan?'

'I'd definitely like to.'

'After your next collection I can do big interview with
you?'

'That would be nice. Thank you very much.'

While the Pebble Mill crew is being wheeled on by Ros, Bruce is waving to friends in the crowd and to the workroom girls watching him from the sidelines. Ms Lomas wants to know how long he worked on the clothes for the show.

'Months! And up to two minutes before we were a couple of girls short, so Dovanna and Gail were last-minute additions. And Dovanna is six feet two, so everything was too short. The skirts were up to here! The fur coat became a fur jacket!'

'Tell me a little bit about the philosophy behind the collection.'

'Just glamour, sex, comfort, warmth, shape, luxury.'

'If you had to add one item to a woman's wardrobe to update it for autumn, what would it be?'

'An exercise bike!'

Interviews over, Bruce suddenly slumps: the anti-climax bites. 'God, I'm speeding. I need a cigarette. I need a drink. I'm exhausted. It's such a low . . . can you imagine?'

Ahead are the 7.30 reception for designers and foreign buyers at Lancaster House as guests of Peter Morrison, Minister of State for Trade, and the party that Anita and George have arranged for Bruce at San Lorenzo at 10.00: some thirty friends and colleagues will go, including Hazel Collins, Marie Helvin, Sally Brampton, editor of British *Elle*, and Colin Barnes, the illustrator who taught Bruce at St Martin's and divined his early talent. Bruce had thought he might go to the Chenil Galleries and buy a painting this afternoon. Instead, he will go home with the video, playing it over and over again while he tries to assess the collection from every point of view. Accumulated tiredness and tension will make it impossible to relax for another twelve hours.

Marie Helvin:

Model's Eye View

It's inevitable that the backstage atmosphere puts a strain on designers. They're keeping tabs on so many different things. Bruce tries to be calmer than most I know. He doesn't like you to see him upset, so he acts Mr Cool. But he's having to think about what the models look like, whether they are happy with what they're wearing, everyone screaming for his attention, the panic about the audience – will they all show up? There are girls climbing into his dresses, ever-present security men, make-up artists and hairdressers rushing back and forth, and dressers hunting for things dropped on the floor. It's very stressful.

I care about how Bruce feels, and I know what he's going through. So I give him support, tell him things are wonderful, do all I can to boost his mood.

A model has to adapt herself to a collection, because she is projecting the designer's image in order to sell the clothes. She needs to feel good to do this. Like all women, she has her preferences about what suits her. Although this doesn't happen for me with Bruce's clothes, at other shows I haven't always been happy with what I've been given to wear, and in the backstage atmosphere, this can upset your equilibrium. But if you are professional, you fight to control it. I have a simple solution – don't look in the mirror *at all*!

There's a backstage tradition which helps psych you up and calms the nerves – the designer always gives his models champagne.

My number one rule is always to take a look at the stage before I go on. At Bruce's show I wasn't able to do this, because by the time I arrived from the previous show, the audience were already coming in. When I got out there, I found to my surprise there was a step, and I

nearly fell when I set off down the catwalk. But I
carried it off! As soon as I came off I rushed backstage
and said, hey everyone – there's a step out there! Any
model would do this. You help each other out.

I had trouble with the last-minute changes. One of the
models was too big in the bust for the evening dress that
had been chosen for her, and she was bursting out all
over the place, so I wore the dress instead. It was
lovely, but the cups were too big for me, and the dresser
was hunting for Kleenex tissues to pad me out, and
there weren't any to be found. In the end we used the
tissue paper out of the shoe boxes. I really needed to
check myself in the mirror to make sure I wasn't going
to shed tissue the moment I got out on stage. But with
only two mirrors, everyone was trying to check their
appearance at the same time, and suddenly Bruce and
George were shouting at me, c'mon, c'mon, you're on
next, so I had to go out desperately hoping that
everything would stay in place!

When I'm on the catwalk, I never hear the music. I don't
think music matters to most models. You are too busy
pacing yourself, watching for your turn. You are quite
separate from the other girls, but there is an etiquette.
I'll slow down if I see the girl ahead taking more time at
the end of the runway. This is where the most important
journalists plus the film crews sit, and when a model
gets there she has to stop and show every angle of what
she's wearing. If the photographers start taking extra
pictures, it's important to prolong the chances of getting
the shot.

If you are a really professional model, you *care* about
the clothes. A good model has to know how to wear
them. There is a way of carrying this off so that, to the
people watching, they look as if they belong to you.

You project comfort and confidence. I think for the designer this is the model's most important skill. There is no set 'walk' – in fact you move as you would do normally – but there are certain little tricks, like how to take a jacket off. I'm not the kind of model who can just go and do a show, be paid, and that's the end of it. I am inspired by a designer. I want to help them because I know how hard they have worked and what their show means to them. Everything comes together at the end, when the designer comes out and the crowd cheers. I feel marvellous then, and the mood carries on and on.

All the models I know love working for Bruce, because he is so good to them. He's very generous with his clothes, but he has an extra edge, which is felt by his customers just as much as his models, and this is his love of women, their bodies and all the different shapes and sizes. Everybody likes to flirt with him! What he looks for in a model is glamour and sex. He prefers dark-haired women and black models, and doesn't use fair girls very often. I've worked with Bruce since 1974, and I adore the confidence and authority of his clothes. It's not fashion as statement. When you wear them, the message is *you*. He has a very feminine, sophisticated ideal, and I've seen him inspired by the films of Bette Davis, Joan Crawford and Norma Shearer. He is conquering the American market now, and I'm sure he will do well there.

15

AFTERMATH

BRUCE OLDFIELD

Ninety-eight garments in twenty minutes? How could
it be a success? OK, it looked fine and the audience
seemed to like it, but for me there were too many details
that went wrong because we didn't have time to work
on them. When we took the collection to Singapore in
May and to Aspen, Colorado, in June, the shows worked
beautifully because we rehearsed and rehearsed until
we got it right. Whereas we weren't allowed to use
Cadogan Hall the previous night, and everything had
to be done in a period of three hours.
If I am going to parade my clothes on the runway they
have to look just right. I need to line the models up in
a row and say that doesn't look right on Michelle, swap

with Jane. Even if we had time to do that on Saturday morning it would have screwed up Mikel's running order, he wouldn't have known what to do when the wrong girl came out, and the dressers would have lost their place. So you leave it alone, you let it go. You haven't got much choice.

Ten minutes into the show things were going wrong backstage because we couldn't get the girls dressed quickly enough. So belts weren't tied up properly, some of the jewellery was left off, there were clothes all over the floor. One of the jersey dresses came out with the drape hanging down the wrong side. There was no time to take it off and put it right because the music is pretaped, and if a girl doesn't come out with her music, then she doesn't come out at all. There was one girl who had really big hips. Maybe I didn't use the tape measure as carefully as I should have done at the initial casting because I liked her face. Anyway, I had to change her outfit over and she went out in a suit with a full peplum which covered the hips. Mikel didn't know what was going on. I think the make-up looked good, the hair wasn't bad, and to give them credit, the models managed to look so serene on the runway you'd never know the kind of chaos that was going on backstage.

Our worst moments were caused by the three girls who didn't turn up. Pat Cleveland not coming over was a disaster. The agency supplied us with a substitute who fortunately was great, but that's the kind of thing that can really screw things up. And we had to reorganise the show at the last minute, the places where the girls come in, some on their own, others in groups. That was more worry for Mikel.

Then there are the best models, the ones that never let you down. Marie Helvin gets the audience applauding every time, and when they set off down the catwalk, Hazel Collins and Jane Spencer move like they're angels from heaven.

Getting the balance of the show right is my particular problem, and I still don't know if I pulled it off. There are two elements. Did I manage to make a clear-enough difference between day wear – special occasion day – and evening? Those velvet suits with bugle bead stitching looked great on the catwalk, but no one knew whether they were day or night, and they proved to be difficult to make up so we dropped them anyway after the show. The gold tweed numbers didn't sell very well, perhaps for the same reason.

You are not just providing a spectacular. It's easy enough to do that – you just send out quantities of the same dress in a dazzling colour. But I'm also showing a working collection that I can sell in my shop and to retailers with boutiques abroad who can buy in depth across a lot of different outfits. At my prices it just isn't viable to show a dozen of each dress, and the buyers certainly don't want their customers to turn up at some party in Dallas or Michigan wearing the same frock! They must have a variety of styles to choose from. Those velvet and mink dresses really are couture outfits which ought to come out on the catwalk one by one and stand on their own – but of course there wasn't time. The finale was all wrong because too many applause-worthy dresses all came out at the same time and were lost in a crowd.

The successes were the jersey dresses which sold very well – *Vogue* photographed one and the Princess of Wales ordered one before the show. The lamés went down well with the buyers, who tend to be creatures of habit. The medieval velvet, which was my favourite of the whole collection, was the most photographed and sold fairly well, retailing at about £2,200. The ruched velvet torso with a full taffeta bell skirt just goes on and on. My winged and ruched evening dress was photographed in the *New York Times* and *Harpers,* the Victoria and Albert Museum have it in their collection – and then it didn't sell! You can never be certain of your best sellers.

The section that got the most applause and sold extremely well was the group of petrol-sequinned prints. The only trouble was that the red gel on the lights made it too dark for the photographers to take their pictures.

One final point is that the previous shows caused us a problem by starting late. Anita told me we missed out on quite a few buyers who assumed our show had finished by the time they came out. So there weren't as many trade people there as we wanted. The following week was, as always, very busy for Anita: she saw eight buyers the next day, and that went on all week. But even though the season was very successful, you can't judge whether you've missed out on sales as a result of something like that.

With all the money, effort and time you pour into the creation of a collection, it's a crime if that collection is not shown to its best advantage on the big day. I am coming to realise that the pressures of producing a show at an unknown location without time for proper rehearsals make it very difficult to achieve the standard of production I require.

MIKEL ROSEN

When I began producing shows I used to be backstage,
looking through a peephole. After that I got a TV
monitor. Now I stay out front, seeing the show as the
audience does. I direct from the back of the audience,
talking on the headset to the lighting and music
technicians and to Russell backstage.

The biggest problem with this show for me was the
lighting. First, the power wasn't turned on early
enough – we were still waiting at 7.15 a.m. Then when
we had rehearsed it all as far as we could in the time
allowed, Pebble Mill moved in with their TV cameras.

They objected to the mirror panels set up at the head of the catwalk. They said our moving spotlights would reflect and dazzle the cameras, causing a blind-out and killing the picture. The way round that was for us to up the lighting level all round, which made nonsense of our planning. The first thing that had to go was our idea of a row of black silhouettes against the light, introducing each group of clothes before the model walked down the runway. The velvet and fur dresses in the finale were meant to be seen in a dark moody light, and instead they were bathed in a brilliant white light. Normally, when we make a video or a TV show we film that first with the big lights, and use a different kind of lighting altogether for the live show.

So I had that headache, and because of all the last-minute lighting changes, I had to talk the technicians through everything during the show, rather than just directing them.

I'm used to Fashion Week and making do without rehearsal time, making the best of what you've got. It is particularly hard to put on a well-organised show because some models fly in from abroad the night before and never have a fitting. It's inevitable that one or two of them will have to change outfits at the last moment, and that is usually what is behind chaotic backstage scenes.

Then there are the models who turn up too late for a run-through – or don't turn up at all. I was in my office way after midnight rewriting the running order and changing scenes. There are models who drop in at the last moment and have to be told, 'You've missed the run-through so just listen to Russell before you go on and do exactly what he tells you.' The trouble is when Russell is telling them there are some who are far more interested in their lips and their hair and they aren't concentrating. Then they go out, ignore the lighting which is set up for them to pose against the back wall for eight seconds, and start straight off down the runway. So the lighting technicians are going crazy, the model finishes her turn too early, and the music tape goes out of synch. Meanwhile, a last-minute substitute for a model who doesn't turn up can turn out to be more suitable for Culture Shock than Bruce Oldfield. On top of all this, the changing-room we had in Cadogan Hall was much too small for the number of models. It was so much easier to organise that later showing of the collection in Aspen, where Bruce presented his selection of the best British fashion designers to the American audience. We had two dressing-rooms, one each side of the catwalk, and a central room between them for entering the runway. No fashion show is without problems. Aspen was a triumph, but the crate of Katherine Hamnett's clothes was diverted to the wrong airport. We had to fill the scene somehow, so Bruce dressed the girls in black and white T-shirts which he slashed and scissored in different ways, and in the surprising way these things sometimes happen it looked great and the audience loved it.

With all the problems that crop up in Fashion Week I could have taken the easy way out and done the same as everyone else. I could have thrown six girls out at a time, all entering right and exiting left, but I don't think that is good enough for clothes like these. Although it was a great strain on all of us and we can see the problems I think we produced a different kind of show which stood out to advantage.

VERDICTS

BRITISH PRESS

SALLY
BRAMPTON,
editor of British Elle
It was such a good
collection – grown-up
sophisticated glamour
done really well, and
never pushed so far that it
went over the top.
Fabulous if you have the
money to spend.
I love his clothes but I
think they take some
wearing. They are
dressing-up clothes, and
with all the dressing down
we do I think we are ready
for that. This collection
was all about sex and
shape, but he got the
balance right so that it had
equal appeal to younger
and older generations.
I noticed that he has
tailored, directed and
marketed his day wear
very carefully towards
the American market,
which makes it for me
fractionally less desirable
than the glam and witty
evening wear.

AMERICAN PRESS

BERNARDINE MORRIS,
fashion editor of the New York Times

Bruce Oldfield has recognised that lifestyle designing is THE new direction. He has a life in mind which appeals to the American Yuppy and the wealthy Englishwoman, which takes in entertaining for your husband's business, sitting on charity boards and a great many formal events. He's good at explaining his philosophy, and the consumer today wants information before she buys – no question! So having his voice-over at the show educating us about his philosophy was a big plus. For myself, I always find his matt jerseys the most seductive. I loved them ten years ago when I first saw his show, and now they're even better.

LONDON STORE

CLARE STUBBS,
then buying executive for Harvey Nichols, now fashion director, Harrods

Having known Bruce since the early seventies, I have been able to watch him evolve progressively. He has arrived at the point where he totally understands women and how to accentuate and disguise the female form so that a Bruce Oldfield dress gives a woman total confidence.

As you would expect, the winter collection is sexy and wearable and reflects the current fashion direction, particularly with regard to the soft draped jerseys which we know we can sell so well. Personally I loved the silver pleated lamés, but we tended to buy the expensive highlight numbers such as the gold bullion dresses because we know they will look great in the Christmas windows.

AMERICAN BUYER

LINDA DRESNER
of the Linda Dresner shops,
Park Avenue, New York
and Troy, Michigan
This is our second season buying Bruce Oldfield, and they sold very well last time.

This fall collection seemed even more original and assured than before. Along with the beautiful making and the cool classic feeling you get a little twist which makes the clothes modern and different. I'd almost call it couture. That makes it strong for our customers who are looking for very special evening dresses – something more than the normal pretty tops and skirts. There is a gap in the US market where grand evening dresses ought to be. Times may be tough but we still entertain, we do dress up, we do go to a lot of formal events. And Bruce Oldfield's clothes are flattering to women of any age as long as they are in good shape, and most of us do exercise and diet and take care of ourselves. We bought a few late-day jersey dresses, and quite a few 'robes de châteaux'. Not that we have any *châteaux*, but the concept is there! I'm talking about those black crêpe dresses with gold bullion decoration, the big billowing taffeta skirts and the petrol-coloured sequin group, not just because they were so eye-catching but because they come in a great variety of jackets and skirts so that the customer can choose what looks best for her individually.

Of course couture finish means couture prices, but I think it's money well spent and I believe our customers will think so too. And all the signs are that Bruce Oldfield is at a new beginning in the US.

AMERICAN AGENT

LUCY SHLAFER, *director of M. Shlafer Associates Incorporated for Bruce Oldfield in the USA*

The stores here in the States are very heavily inventoried at this time – in other words, they have a lot of stock that isn't moving. For complicated socio-economic reasons customers have become cautious and they aren't buying as much from their stores as they were four or five seasons ago. So, taking into account the current state of the US market, I would say that Bruce Oldfield is gaining ground more consistently, and it is a solid building process with buyers coming back each time for more.

When the high fashion market is changing perspective, as it is at present, it's interesting that some of Bruce's biggest orders are coming from areas hardest hit by the oil crisis, such as Houston and Dallas. There is a real need for, and interest in, evening wear for an elite society, and Bruce is capable of providing the fantasy that's wanted. He particularly appeals to the body-conscious, fit American woman of all types and ages, and he has been quick to pick up special points that will attract her. For instance, his colouration and fabrication is now well targeted for US sales; he also makes a point of necklines that show off jewellery to advantage. Bruce is associated with the Princess of Wales here, but his dresses stand up well on their own. I would put it like this: so far, so good.

ANITA RICHARDSON

This collection was a landmark for us, a major leap in exporting Bruce Oldfield clothes on a world-wide scale, after the years concentrating on couture. It was a success. As our main outlets in Britain are our own shop and Harvey Nichols, we look to the American buyers for our big orders. In the days that followed the show, I was seeing up to sixteen buyers a day. Despite initial press coverage and feedback from those buyers, I could not be sure of our success until the orders started coming through over the next months. There seems to be little rhyme or reason behind the stores' buying habits. Sometimes the lines they take the previous season sell extremely well for them, yet their buyers don't appear for even a brief look. At other times, company politics come into play. Six or eight people from the same store came in together that week and made a lot of noise, but reached no decision. They all had different opinions, and it was impossible for them to agree. I play things by ear. I don't believe in being aggressive and twisting people's arms. I would much rather they buy ten or twelve outfits, and sell them all, than buy eighteen and sell only twelve. It's the unsold stock that buyers remember.

We sold to boutiques in America, Australia, Singapore and Hong Kong. The boutique buyer is often also the owner. She has no one to please other than herself and her clients. She tends to buy at the more expensive end of a collection, so I can be more confident of orders here. We had an excellent order, for example, from the American boutique owner Linda Dresner. After London Fashion Week, the collection was shipped to our agents in

New York for display in their showrooms. The tension really began there for me, because although Lucy Shlafer rang me regularly and reported lots of numbers going into little black books, the orders didn't come through until a few weeks later. It was when I saw our telex machine suddenly become very busy that I knew it wasn't all talk. What is happening now is that the American buyers are regarding our shows here as previews. They like to get back home, see what other people are doing, work out their budgets, get the OK from their merchandise directors and then place their orders. Even then there are delays because our agent there has to deal with the credit ratings. She sees that the money is confirmed through the banks. The whole filtering process takes five weeks. process takes five weeks. One of the problems with export is that you have to get the colourations and fabrics right for all climates from Singapore to Canada, taking account of facts you learn from experience, such as the way big cities tend to order laid-back colours and the West Coast and hotter climates prefer bright colours. Some years all your orders come from Europe and you realise you haven't offered enough variety. But this year the order book is filled from the widest variety of cities and countries. That's one of the things that make us feel we've got it right this time. Since this collection, the Virginia Slims company have been using our clothes in their advertising, and it's increased our profile in the States. The advertising industry there has a strong influence, and as we are credited, it's one more factor making Bruce Oldfield clothes internationally known. I will not have complete figures for our financial year until next year, but the previous figures showed a big leap in profit and turnover. This year we have added to that, because the orders after this collection topped £200,000. Quite simply, we have really taken off on an international level. This will certainly be our most successful year to date.

PICTURES BY NEIL KIRK

17

EPILOGUE

Friday 4 April

It is one of the rare quiet periods of the year at Argon Mews. The workroom is tidy and serene. Radio 4 plays while the machinists finish up the private customers' outfits that have been held over from before the collection, including the silk dresses and suits on order for Ascot week. Anita is on holiday in Morocco, and George has spent the morning looking for white satin shoes. Her wedding is on 19 April, and her wedding dress is, naturally, by Bruce Oldfield. Bruce has spent some of the week flat-hunting, looking in antique shops and art galleries, and buying Armani suits in South Molton Street. This afternoon he is back in the studio pinning shirred silk to a stand. He is in an unusually reflective mood, partly because it is just over a decade since he set up his company with that borrowed £1,500. It is a sum which will buy just one of his evening dresses today.

'Being labelled a success too early can be a disadvantage,' he says. 'Once that has happened you have to be able to follow through, because the fashion business is all about continuity. It is very hard to be stuck with a reputation, as I was, when you have just left college and before you know anything about running a business. What really counts is staying power. It gives me a lot of pleasure to say that I have a properly established business now. There are about thirty-six people employed under my name, and we are here to stay. So now I'm looking ahead to the next collection. The show is the heart of the season, the source of some of the greatest satisfaction – and the greatest pain. My reaction afterwards is always the same – never again! Never, ever again!'

At this moment George puts her head round the door to say, 'We've just got the tickets for Frankfurt, by the way. It's 15 to 18 April.'

'There you go,' says Bruce. 'I've just said never again, and in only eleven days' time I'll be starting the whole circus off once more, choosing summer fabrics at Interstoff. That's what I mean by continuity.'

ACKNOWLEDGEMENTS

In gratitude to Philip Norman for his support and help, and to Deborah Beale for all her painstaking work.

Thanks also to Georgina Alexander-Sinclair for patience and helpfulness beyond the call of duty.

In gratitude to Philip Norman for his support and help, to Deborah Beale for all her painstaking work, and to Georgina Alexander-Sinclair for showing uncharacteristic patience and resolve throughout.

Art direction by Lamb and Shirley. Designed by Valerie Wickes and Tim Lamb. Photographs of the company at work by Alan Wickes.

The following pictures are reproduced by kind permission of the copyright holders: all material is the copyright of the people or publications named.

Pages 11, 73, 229, 230, 231, 232 and 233: courtesy of *Vogue*/The Condé Nast Publications Ltd

Page 40: *The Times*

Pages 55, 226–32: Neil Kirk

Page 74: (1) Press Association Photographs, (2) Syndication International Ltd, (3) Press Association Photographs

Page 75: Press Association Photographs

Page 76: (1) Eva Sereny, (2) The *Sun*

Page 77: (1) Rex Features Ltd, (2) Alan Bond

Page 208: David Bailey

The picture of Bruce Oldfield appearing on page 12 and throughout chapter 2: Tony McGee

The authors and the publisher wish to thank Island Pictures for their kind permission to reproduce the lines that appear on pages 132 and 190 from the film, *The Kiss of the Spiderwoman*.